THE MONROE DOCTRINE
THE CORNERSTONE OF AMERICAN FOREIGN POLICY

MILESTONES
IN AMERICAN HISTORY

THE MONROE DOCTRINE

THE CORNERSTONE OF AMERICAN FOREIGN POLICY

EDWARD J. RENEHAN JR.

An imprint of Infobase Publishing

Cover: President James Monroe (right) and members of his cabinet discuss the basis of American foreign policy. From left to right: John Quincy Adams, W. H. Crawford, and William Wirt.

The Monroe Doctrine: The Cornerstone of American Foreign Policy

Copyright © 2007 by Infobase Publishing

Chelsea House
An imprint of Infobase Publishing
132 West 31st Street
New York, NY 10001

ISBN-10: 0-7910-9353-0
ISBN-13: 978-0-7910-9353-5

Library of Congress Cataloging-in-Publication Data
Renehan, Edward, 1956-
  The Monroe doctrine : the cornerstone of American foreign policy /
Edward J. Renehan Jr.
     p. cm. — (Milestones in American history)
  Includes bibliographical references and index.
  ISBN 0-7910-9353-0 (hardcover)
  1. Monroe doctrine. I. Title. II. Series.

  JZ1482.R46 2007
  327.7304—dc22
              2006034126

Chelsea House books are available at special discounts when purchased in bulk quantities for businesses, associations, institutions, or sales promotions. Please call our Special Sales Department in New York at (212) 967-8800 or (800) 322-8755.

You can find Chelsea House on the World Wide Web at http://www.chelseahouse.com

Series design by Erik Lindstrom
Cover design by Ben Peterson

Printed in the United States of America

BANG NMSG 10 9 8 7 6 5 4 3 2 1

This book is printed on acid-free paper.

All links and Web addresses were checked and verified to be correct at the time of publication. Because of the dynamic nature of the Web, some addresses and links may have changed since publication and may no longer be valid.

CONTENTS

Key
Pronouncement

Article II, Section 3, of the U.S. Constitution states that "The President shall from time to time give to Congress information of the State of the Union and recommend to their Consideration such measures as he shall judge necessary and expedient."

On a cold January morning in 1790, President George Washington rode in a carriage drawn by six horses from his residence on Cherry Street in New York City to Federal Hall. There, waiting for him, gathered both houses of Congress— the House of Representatives and the Senate—to whom Washington delivered a strident and optimistic speech.

By personally delivering this first annual message to Congress, Washington believed he was setting a precedent for his successors. But in fact, since that first "State of the Union," the message's length, frequency, and method of delivery have varied from president to president and from decade to decade. Presidents have always used the message to present their particular goals and agendas and to rally support for themselves. But formats and rituals have shifted dramatically through the years.

For example, Thomas Jefferson thought Washington's oral presentation was too kingly for the new republic. Likewise, Jefferson found Congress's practice of giving a courteous reply in person at the president's residence to be too formal as well. Thus, Jefferson detailed his priorities in his first annual State of the Union message in 1801 in the form of a written document, copies of which were sent to each house of Congress. The president's annual message, as it was then called, would not be spoken by a president for the next 112 years. (In fact, the first president to revive Washington's spoken approach would be Woodrow Wilson in 1913.)

MESSENGER WITH A MESSAGE

So it was that President James Monroe's seventh State of the Union address—"delivered" on December 2, 1823—was neither recited nor read aloud, but rather dispatched via courier. It was an unusually bitter early December afternoon. Monroe's messenger wore a scarf and gloves as he rode down Pennsylvania Avenue on a fine black horse, which was a resident of the Executive Mansion stables. No one walking along the street took particular notice of the man. And certainly, no one would have guessed the importance or the historic nature of the document he carried under his arm. The messenger's package included several folds of paper bearing a score of mundane paragraphs alluding to such trivial matters as postal regulations and affairs of taxation. But the document also contained language that would change American diplomatic procedure, practice, and history through the decades to come.

The messenger and his horse mingled easily and naturally with other riders bound on the most commonplace of errands.

VIEW OF WASHINGTON.

During the first part of the nineteenth century, the U.S. Capitol looked significantly different than the current Capitol. The building changed dramatically in the 1850s, when the original timber-framed dome was replaced and the wings expanded.

There seemed nothing particularly remarkable about the rider from James Monroe's office, and indeed there was nothing remarkable about him except for his package. Even this seemed of no particularly unique importance: just another yearly summary and wish list dispatched from the chief executive to the members of the Senate and the House of Representatives; just another opening bid in the bartering game that defined American politics.

Arriving at the Capitol building, the messenger hitched his horse to a post and began moving up the steps to the main entrance, his package still under his arm. The building he approached looked significantly different than today's Capitol.

The dome was short and squat, and the wings did not extend as far as they do today. Indeed, the building Monroe's messenger went to was in a state of reconstruction, having been partially burned by British troops during the War of 1812. The noted architect Benjamin Latrobe had been principally connected with the original construction and many innovative interior features. But now, since his death in 1820, the work was being carried on by his equally famous and talented successor, Charles Bulfinch.

Once inside the main foyer of the elaborate building, the messenger made his way first to the Senate chambers and then to the chambers of the House, dropping his packages off with the president of the Senate (Monroe's vice president, Daniel D. Tompkins of New York) and the speaker of the House of Representatives (Henry Clay of Kentucky, founder of the Whig Party.) Thereafter, the messenger turned on his heel, strode out of the Capitol building, remounted his horse, and returned the way he had come, up Pennsylvania Avenue, to the offices and home of President Monroe.

MATTERS DIPLOMATIC AND OTHERWISE

"Many important subjects will claim your attention during the present session, of which I shall endeavor to give, in aid of your deliberations, a just idea in this communication." So James Monroe began his seventh message to Congress. He continued:

> I undertake this duty with diffidence, from the vast extent of the interests on which I have to treat and of their great importance to every portion of our Union. I enter on it with zeal from a thorough conviction that there never was a period since the establishment of our Revolution when, regarding the condition of the civilized world and its bearing on us, there was greater necessity for devotion in the public servants to their respective duties, or for virtue, patriotism, and union in our constituents. . . .

The people being with us exclusively the sovereign, it is indispensable that full information be laid before them on all important subjects, to enable them to exercise that high power with complete effect. If kept in the dark, they must be incompetent to it. We are all liable to error, and those who are engaged in the management of public affairs are more subject to excitement and to be led astray by their particular interests and passions than the great body of our constituents, who, living at home in the pursuit of their ordinary avocations, are calm but deeply interested spectators of events and of the conduct of those who are parties to them.

From here, Monroe went on to report the progress of various U.S. diplomats negotiating under articles contained within the Treaty of Ghent, the 1814 document that had concluded the War of 1812. Many years after the end of that conflict, U.S. and British representatives continued to bicker over the boundary between the United States and Canada. After summarizing these talks, the president also announced to Congress a new round of negotiations with the British toward establishing a treaty that would define the exclusive and shared commercial interests of the United States and Great Britain as regarded states and territories bordering on lakes and rivers emptying into the St. Lawrence River.

Monroe further reported on various negotiations with France, and negotiations with the Russian Imperial Government regarding the respective rights and interests of Russia and the United States on the northwest coast of North America.

THE MONROE DOCTRINE

Having summed up the current diplomatic situation, Monroe enunciated the policy that would hereafter be known as the Monroe Doctrine: "In the discussions to which this interest has given rise and in the arrangements by which they may terminate the occasion has been judged proper for asserting, as a principle in which the rights and interests of the United States are involved, that the American continents, by the free and independent condition which they have assumed and maintain, are henceforth not to be considered as subjects for future colonization by any European powers."

Such a doctrine would need a strong navy to back it up, and this—Monroe assured Congress—they had. "The usual force has been maintained in the Mediterranean Sea, the Pacific Ocean, and along the Atlantic coast, and has afforded the necessary protection to our commerce in those seas," Monroe wrote. He continued:

> In the West Indies and the Gulf of Mexico our naval force has been augmented by the addition of several small vessels provided for by the "act authorizing an additional naval force for the suppression of piracy," passed by Congress at their last session. That armament has been eminently successful in the accomplishment of its object. The piracies by which our commerce in the neighborhood of the island of Cuba had been afflicted have been repressed and the confidence of our merchants in a great measure restored. . . . Although our expedition, cooperating with an invigorated administration of the government of the island of Cuba, and with the corresponding active exertions of a British naval force in the same seas, have almost entirely destroyed the unlicensed piracies from that island, the success of our exertions has not been equally effectual to suppress the same crime, under other pretenses and colors, in the neighboring island of Puerto Rico. They have been committed there under the abusive issue of Spanish commissions. . . .
>
> It is a source of great satisfaction that we are always enabled to recur to the conduct of our Navy with price and commendation as a means of national defense it enjoys the public confidence, and is steadily assuming additional importance. It is submitted whether a more efficient and

James Monroe was elected the fifth president of the United States in 1816 and would go on to serve two terms (1817 to 1825). During his second term, Monroe introduced the Monroe Doctrine, which would become the cornerstone of U.S. foreign policy well into the twentieth century.

equally economical organization of it might not in several respects be effected. It is supposed that higher grades than now exist by law would be useful. They would afford well-merited rewards to those who have long and faithfully served their country, present the best incentives to good conduct, and the best means of insuring a proper discipline; destroy the inequality in that respect between military and naval services, and relieve our officers from many inconveniences and mortifications which occur when our vessels meet those of other nations, ours being the only service in which such grades do not exist.

Summing up, Monroe added:

The citizens of the United States cherish sentiments the most friendly in favor of the liberty and happiness of their fellow men on [the other] side of the Atlantic. In the wars of the European powers in matters relating to themselves we have never taken any part, nor does it comport with our policy so to do. It is only when our rights are invaded or seriously menaced that we resent injuries or make preparation for our defense. With the movements in this hemisphere we are of necessity more immediately connected, and by causes which must be obvious to all enlightened and impartial observers . . . . We owe it, therefore, to candor and to the amicable relations existing between the United States and those powers to declare that we should consider any attempt on their part to extend their system to any portion of this hemisphere as dangerous to our peace and safety. With the existing colonies or dependencies of any European power we have not interfered and shall not interfere, but with the Governments who have declared their independence and maintained it, and whose independence we have, on great consideration and on just principles, acknowledged, we could not view any interposition for the purpose of oppressing them, or controlling in any other manner their destiny, by any European power in any other light than as the manifestation of an unfriendly disposition toward the United States. . . .

Our policy in regard to Europe, which was adopted at an early stage of the wars which have so long agitated that quarter of the globe, nevertheless remains the same, which is, not to interfere in the internal concerns of any of its powers; to consider the government de facto as the legitimate government for us; to cultivate friendly relations with it, and to preserve those relations by a frank, firm, and manly policy, meeting in all instances the just claims of every power, submitting to injuries from none.

But in regard to those continents circumstances are eminently and conspicuously different. It is impossible that the allied powers should extend their political system to any portion of either continent without endangering our peace and happiness; nor can anyone believe that our southern brethren, if left to themselves, would adopt it of their own accord. It is equally impossible, therefore, that we should behold such interposition in any form with indifference. If we look to the comparative strength and resources of Spain and those new Governments, and their distance from each other, it must be obvious that she can never subdue them. It is still the true policy of the United States to leave the parties to themselves, in the hope that other powers will pursue the same course.

FEW WORDS, MAJOR IMPACT

Monroe's words were few. However, they enunciated a philosophy of the American sphere of influence in the Western Hemisphere that exists to the present day, and that has shaped the foreign policies of every president since. James Monroe's secretary of state, John Quincy Adams, who played a major role in defining the doctrine, viewed the statement as a deterrent to colonialism generally. Ironically, however, during the late twentieth century, the Monroe Doctrine would be used to justify CIA infiltration and manipulation of sovereign states in Latin America, including Chile and Nicaragua. Prior to that, it was also used by President Theodore Roosevelt at the start of the twentieth century to defend South America against intervention by rival European powers, while at the same time legitimizing the United States' own unique form of colonialism in those quarters.

As Henry Kissinger—secretary of state under presidents Richard Nixon and Gerald Ford—has said:

> No single utterance of an American president, no statement of policy and strategic political philosophy, has had more influence on the history of the world and the history of a region than President James Monroe's fundamental and seminal statement of 1823. Simultaneously, no doctrine has been more cynically abused, redefined, and redesigned to meet the changing needs and priorities of different presidential administrations. Always, has the self-interest of the United States governed the interpretation and application of the idealistic words put down on paper by James Monroe and John Quincy Adams, and always shall that be the case. Although the core language of the Monroe Doctrine has not changed over time, the methods and the motivations of the American diplomats deploying and defending that Doctrine most certainly have, and will again, more than once, in the future. Count on that.

American Diplomacy and Foreign Policy, 1789–1817

Several decades of American foreign policy helped formulate the ideas behind the Monroe Doctrine. James Monroe was the nation's fifth president. Each of his four predecessors possessed his own priorities and style when it came to dealing with foreign powers. This chapter serves as an introduction to review foreign policy under presidents Washington, Adams, Jefferson, and Madison, spanning the years 1789 to 1817.

FOREIGN POLICY UNDER GEORGE WASHINGTON (1789–1797)

Being the first president of the United States, it was incumbent upon George Washington to set foreign policy precedents. After all, because he was the first president, it was impossible for him not to lay the groundwork for the future. In all matters of foreign relations, Washington sought—as every executive after him

During President George Washington's two terms as president, the United States adopted a policy of isolationism, because the country was too weak to become embroiled in the affairs of foreign countries. Washington, who is depicted in this 1795 oil painting by American artist Rembrandt Peale, focused on building up the U.S. Navy and negotiating treaties with foreign nations during his presidency.

always would—to seize and centralize as much power as possible in the executive branch. First, Washington set the precedent of the executive branch administering treaty negotiations when he approached the Creek Nation of American Indians, looking for congressional approval only after the fact. Washington also seized the initiative in sending American representatives overseas for negotiations without consulting Congress.

Foreign intrigue and complications dominated Washington's two-term presidency from the start. Many Americans—being generally supportive of the ideals of the 1789 French Revolution, and also annoyed at British attempts to incite Native Americans against settlers in the western border region of the United States—believed the United States should aid France in any conflict with Great Britain. Washington, however, refused to make such a commitment, because he realized that the young United States—in the wake of the American Revolution—was simply too weak at that moment to become involved in foreign wars. Thus Washington's insistence on neutrality set yet another key precedent, as did his insistence that the power to make such a determination be held by the president.

In 1793, at the start of Washington's second term, France declared war on Great Britain and several other European countries. At home in the United States, debate over how the young country should respond was loud and discordant. Thomas Jefferson (Washington's secretary of state) and Alexander Hamilton (his secretary of the treasury) took opposite sides. Jefferson lobbied for the support of France and Hamilton lobbied for the support of Great Britain, while Washington himself favored neutrality. Meanwhile, the French ambassador to the United States—Edmond Charles Genêt—gave speeches up and down the eastern seaboard, arguing for American intervention on the side of the French. Washington despised Genêt's meddling in American diplomatic issues and anxiously awaited a chance to get rid of him. Washington's opportunity came when the ambassador, disobeying clearly enunciated orders from Washington that forbade French warships to sail from American ports, nevertheless facilitated the arrival and departure of a French privateer in Philadelphia. After this, Washington demanded that the French government recall Genêt.

Early in 1793, the British foreign secretary announced that his government, in the form of the Royal Navy, would disrespect any claims of neutrality on the high seas, and seize any ships (including American vessels) trading with the French. Within a year, this program on the part of the British caused the Americans to virtually halt all trade with foreign ports, while Washington rushed to build up the piteously small U.S. Navy so that it might defend the new nation's rights to foreign trade. During this period, Washington successfully petitioned Congress for the funds to build six warships, among them the USS *Constitution*. At the same time, however, an American representative sent to London to negotiate foreign trade and other matters found himself shunned. Even more alarming: The British began building a fort in the Ohio wilderness and inciting Native Americans in that region to challenge American interests.

Despite these provocations, Washington—mindful of the tenuous standing of the fragile United States in the face of British imperial power—let it be known that he preferred a diplomatic solution to a military one. This announcement, in turn, gave the British the upper hand in negotiations. Washington's envoy to London, John Jay, wound up negotiating a weak treaty that greatly favored British interests. What came to be known as the Jay Treaty did nothing to proclaim American freedom on the high seas with regard to trade. In addition, the treaty did nothing to address impressments (the British practice of seizing American citizens on the high seas and forcing them into service for the British Navy). In time, Congress grudgingly approved the Jay Treaty, and Washington hesitantly signed it while at the same time citing the document as a case study in why a nation-state should always avoid negotiating from a weak position.

(continues on page 18)

In 1794, Chief Justice John Jay (depicted here) negotiated a treaty with Great Britain in which the British agreed to withdraw from the Northwest Territory, cease plundering U.S. trade vessels, and grant the United States trade rights in Great Britain and the British East Indies. In return, the United States agreed to pay off debts to British merchants that were incurred prior to the American Revolution.

GEORGE WASHINGTON'S FAREWELL ADDRESS OF 1796

Although President George Washington's farewell address was his most famous speech, he did not actually deliver it in person. Instead, Washington arranged to have it published on September 19, 1796, in a Philadelphia newspaper. Seven days later, the speech was reprinted by Thomas Adams and Isaac Larkin in Boston's *Independent Chronicle,* which had served as the voice of the Republican Party in New England since 1776. In his "Farewell Address," Washington warns his fellow citizens against becoming embroiled in foreign entanglements:

> Against the insidious wiles of foreign influence (I conjure you to believe me, fellow-citizens), the jealousy of a free people ought to be constantly awake; since history and experience prove, that foreign influence is one of the most baneful foes of Republican Government. But that jealousy, to be useful, must be impartial; else it becomes the instrument of the very influence to be avoided, instead of a defense against it. Excessive partiality for one foreign nation, and excessive dislike of another, cause those whom they actuate to see danger only on one side, and serve to veil and even second the arts of influence on the other. Real patriots, who may resist the intrigues of the favorite, are liable to become suspected and odious; while its tools and dupes usurp the applause and confidence of the people, to surrender their interests.
>
> The great rule of conduct for us, in regard to foreign nations, is, in extending our commercial relations, to have with them as little political connection as possible. So far as we have already formed engagements, let them be fulfilled with perfect good faith. Here let us stop.

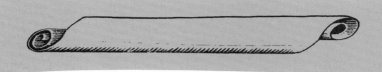

Europe has a set of primary interests, which to us have none, or a very remote relation. Hence she must be engaged in frequent controversies, the causes of which are essentially foreign to our concerns. Hence, therefore, it must be unwise in us to implicate ourselves, by artificial ties, in the ordinary vicissitudes of her politics, or the ordinary combinations and collisions of her friendships or enmities.

Our detached and distant situation invites and enables us to pursue a different course. If we remain one people, under an efficient government, the period is not far off, when we may defy material injury from external annoyance; when we may take such an attitude as will cause the neutrality, we may at any time resolve upon, to be scrupulously respected; when belligerent nations, under the impossibility of making acquisitions upon us, will not lightly hazard the giving us provocation; when we may choose peace or war, as our interest, guided by justice, shall counsel.

Why forego the advantages of so peculiar a situation? Why quit our own to stand upon foreign ground? Why, by interweaving our destiny with that of any part of Europe, entangle our peace and prosperity in the toils of European ambition, rivalship, interest, humor, or caprice?

It is our true policy to steer clear of permanent alliances with any portion of the foreign world; so far, I mean, as we are now at liberty to do it; for let me not be understood as capable of patronizing infidelity to existing engagements. I hold the maxim no less applicable to public than to private affairs, that honesty is always the best policy. I repeat it, therefore, let those engagements be observed in their genuine sense. But, in my opinion, it is unnecessary and would be unwise to extend them.

(continued from page 14)

During the final years of Washington's presidency, the twin foreign focuses of executive attention were the governments of Algiers and Spain. Throughout this period, Algerian pirates from North Africa's Barbary region made a habit of capturing American vessels, plundering their stores and cargo, and kidnapping or killing their crews. In the end, without a capable, full-fledged navy to rely on, Washington wound up negotiating a treaty with the Algerians that constituted little more than the payment of blackmail by the United States. In return for the payment of protection money, the government of Algeria guaranteed the safety of American vessels in Barbary waters. The treaty—which was nothing short of humiliating—made Washington even more intent on building a large, world-class navy. Although Washington himself would not live long enough to see the profitable results of his long-term naval buildup, other presidents would eventually use the ships Washington funded to good advantage in the Barbary region and elsewhere.

Washington's treaty with Spain was much more profitable for the United States. After intense negotiations, the Spanish agreed that their agents in the Spanish-controlled part of Florida would no longer encourage Native American attacks on American settlers north of the border between Florida and Georgia. In addition, Spain granted Americans open access to navigation on the Mississippi River, in this way facilitating settlement and commerce through the bulk of the Ohio River Valley. With the Mississippi open as far south as New Orleans, pelts and agricultural products could now be shipped down the Ohio and Cumberland rivers to the Mississippi, and then to New Orleans for shipment to Europe and other markets.

Meanwhile, John Jay's treaty with the British continued to be a thorn in the side of American diplomacy. France took offense at the document, which it viewed as contradicting the agreements of alliance Louis XVI had signed with diplomats representing the Continental Congress during the American Revolution. By 1796, as a direct result of the Jay Treaty, it was the outraged French that harassed American ships. In time, the Americans and French would actually engage in brief battles on the high seas, although full-scale war would never be declared.

FOREIGN POLICY UNDER JOHN ADAMS (1797–1801)

In 1796, the Federalist John Adams (George Washington's vice president) succeeded Washington as president. Adams had defeated Thomas Jefferson and Thomas Pinckney, the former of which, as the second-highest vote getter, filled the position of vice president. Early in Adams's presidency, the French seized nearly 300 American ships bound for British ports. While leaders of the Federalist Party called for war, Adams attempted a diplomatic solution and sent delegates to France. French agents (code-named X, Y, and Z) demanded a $250,000 bribe and a $12 million loan to France in order to continue negotiations. The American delegates Charles Cotesworth Pinckney, John Marshall, and Elbridge Gerry rejected the demands. In the aftermath of what came to be called the XYZ Affair, avoiding outright war with France soon became Adams's chief foreign policy goal.

Like Washington, Adams realized the young republic was in no way prepared for war. Also like Washington, who had tended to focus on naval matters despite his own land-based military resume, Adams favored the building up of the navy and collateral work to construct coastal defenses at such strategic locations as the entrances to harbors. However, another school of politicians, led by Adams's fellow Federalist (and former secretary of the treasury) Alexander Hamilton, instead lobbied Congress to fund a large standing army. When Congress agreed, Hamilton had himself named the army's inspector general.

Despite Hamilton's maneuvering and diversion of funds that otherwise would have gone to strengthening the navy to defend American shipping against incursions by Algerian pirates and the French, Adams nevertheless still found success in treaty talks with France. During February 1799, he sent several peace commissioners to Paris to discuss peace. This action on Adams's part was a response to diplomatic overtures from the French foreign minister, Charles Maurice de Talleyrand-Périgord, indicating that the French government was ready for serious negotiations. In the course of these discussions, Secretary of State Timothy Pickering, a close protégé of Hamilton, tried to derail productive talks and Adams wound up demanding his resignation. After this brief bump in the road, however, the French and American delegations came to an amicable agreement.

Once the prospect of war with France had been eliminated, Adams had an ideal excuse for dismantling Hamilton's army, which he promptly did. Adams's move at the same time split the Federalist Party into several antagonized factions. The split happened on the eve of the 1800 presidential election. Thus, ironically, Adams's success facilitated his defeat at the polls in favor of the Democratic-Republican Thomas Jefferson, whose party also made inroads in both houses of Congress.

FOREIGN POLICY UNDER THOMAS JEFFERSON (1801–1809)

The most important foreign policy development of Thomas Jefferson's first term was the 1803 purchase of the Louisiana Territory. In fact, this deal—negotiated in Paris by New York's Robert R. Livingston and Virginia's James Monroe—constituted the most notable achievement of Jefferson's entire presidency. While secretary of state under George Washington, Jefferson had devoted a great deal of time and attention toward gaining rights of free navigation of the Mississippi River for American

AUGUST 1804.
BOMBARDMENT OF TRIPOLI.

In 1801, President Thomas Jefferson dispatched the U.S. Navy to present-day Libya in response to the pasha (military leader) of Tripoli's demand that the United States pay more tribute to ensure safe passage of other ships through the Mediterranean Sea. The military action that ensued became known as the Tripolitan War; the first victory for the United States on foreign soil.

citizens. In gaining those rights, he had been aggressive in his dealings with the Kingdom of Spain, and his aggressiveness worked, with Spain granting the sought-after navigation rights. A bit later, however, the situation changed. Control of the province of Louisiana moved from Spain to Napoleonic France, and Jefferson became worried about further French territorial ambitions in North America. Thus, when the French offered to sell the Louisiana Territory in 1803, the American eagerly accepted. The Louisiana Purchase was the acquisition of more than 530,000,000 acres (828,000 square miles) of territory at the cost of about 3 cents per acre.

As important as the Louisiana acquisition was, Jefferson also met with success in other diplomatic efforts. During May 1801, the ruler of Tripoli in North Africa, after noting the protection money being paid to the Algerians by the United States to ensure safety for American vessels, declared war on the United States with the intent of demanding similar protection money. This time, the American response was different. Armed with the fighting ships originally commissioned by Washington, Jefferson ordered a squadron to the Mediterranean, where they blockaded the main harbor of Tripoli. As a result of the successful blockade, Jefferson was able to negotiate a treaty between the United States and Tripoli with terms quite favorable to the Americans.

During Jefferson's second term, the ongoing and increasingly bloody conflict between Great Britain and France—which, by its nature, took place in waters throughout the globe—threatened the position of the neutral United States, a bystander in the affairs of each rival power. In time, both Great Britain and France began—despite previous treaties—to usurp American rights on the open oceans, with Great Britain being the worst offender. The British also continued their policy of boarding American vessels and seizing American seamen, impressing them into service in the Royal Navy. Thus American commerce—and, of course, American dignity—found itself caught in the crossfire between the world's two greatest powers.

Jefferson recognized the complexity of the American position. He could not seek and gain favorable terms with the British without offending and enraging the French. And he could not seek and gain favorable terms with the French without offending and enraging the British. Thus, he sought a middle ground. Rather than cozying up to one power over another, and rather than confronting further insults on the high seas, Jefferson chose a third option. He suspended international commerce between the United States and both Great Britain and France. Jefferson's embargo, adopted in December 1807, represented a drastic step economically, which put great pressure on the national economy. But Jefferson viewed the embargo as a necessary solution: the only alternative between the unattractive options of war and submission. In the end, however, the embargo had less impact on the British and French economies than on the American economy, which it adversely affected, especially in the Federalist stronghold of New England, where desperate merchants, industrialists, and shipowners eventually started ignoring the ban.

Toward the end of his tenure in office, Jefferson grudgingly agreed to end the formal embargo, and Congress eventually adopted a more moderate measure. However, this did nothing to help the United States avoid eventual war with Great Britain, as we will see.

FOREIGN POLICY UNDER JAMES MADISON (1809–1817)

James Madison had served as secretary of state to Jefferson, his friend and fellow Virginian. When Madison came into the presidency, he did so with great allegiance to virtually all Jeffersonian ideals. This was true with regard to both domestic politics and foreign policy.

During the election of 1808, the memory of the embargo cost Madison several electoral votes from New England. Nevertheless, he was easily elected president with votes from the mid-Atlantic and southern states. In Madison, the Democratic-Republican Party found a less energetic leader than what it was used to in Jefferson, and the party itself languished a bit under Madison's less charismatic leadership. Despite Madison's prestige as a statesman, real-world dilemmas—such as the myriad complications in international relations caused by the Napoleonic Wars (1803–1815), wars fought during Napoleon Bonaparte's rule of France—frequently upset the plans and thwarted the most ambitious policies of his administration.

During his first year as president, Madison and Congress continued recent tradition, prohibiting trade with both Great Britain and France. Then, in May 1810, Congress reversed itself: authorizing the president to pursue trade with both countries, provided each accepted America's view of neutral rights, or trade with only one, if that one accepted America's view of neutral rights. Of the two warring parties, only France endeavored to comply. Thus, late in 1810, President Madison declared a state of "non-intercourse" with Great Britain. Simultaneous with this, a young group of congressional "War Hawks," including Henry Clay, John C. Calhoun, and Richard M. Johnson, argued for a declaration of war. Eventually, Great Britain's continued seizure of American ships and cargos, and continued impressment of American seamen, forced Madison to give in to the demands of the hawks. Madison asked Congress for a declaration of war on June 1, 1812.

At first, the war did not go well for the Americans. Madison had a hard time finding capable civilian and military leaders. The U.S. Army proved a particular disappointment. Where Madison had hoped for a victorious incursion into Canada, what he got instead was an ignominious surrender of U.S. troops at Detroit, and another just like it on the Niagara frontier. Occasional naval victories sometimes cheered the American people and their weary president. But American problems financing the war, coupled with French defeats in Europe and further unsuccessful American ground campaigns in 1813, left Madison uncertain of the future.

Madison had begun seeking a diplomatic resolution shortly after the start of the war. In time, Russia offered to mediate, and Madison thus sent delegates to St. Petersburg. Only later, however, did he learn that the British refused to talk through intermediaries. Thus, through channels, it was arranged that both sides would meet in the Belgian town of Ghent for face-to-face negotiations. The meeting took place in August 1814.

From the beginning of the talks, agreement seemed within reach. For starters, the United States dropped its demand that Great Britain end its impressment of American sailors, because the Crown had already agreed to do so. After the defeat of Napoleon's navy at the Battle of Trafalgar in 1805, Great Britain had more ships and sailors than she needed, and was not in the market for more. As for the other major U.S. grievance—British Orders-in-Council forbidding American trade with other European countries—these had already been repealed by Parliament. The only remaining issues were territorial, having to do with the continent of North America. These were easily resolved. Great Britain eventually agreed not to go forward with a proposed barrier-state of Native Americans strategically positioned between the United States and Canada. Thereafter, with that matter settled to the advantage of everyone except the Native Americans, both the United States and Great Britain agreed to end the war.

Signed December 24, 1814, the Treaty of Ghent is, at heart, an ironic document. With neither Great Britain nor the United States gaining any territory or any trade advantage, all the bloodshed in essence seemed pointless. What small advantages either side gained were subtle, to say the least. In the wake of the War of 1812, the United States pushed Native American tribes—formerly the allies of the British—off their traditional lands in the Northwest Territory (the present-day states of Ohio, Indiana, Illinois, Michigan, and Wisconsin) and opened them for white settlement. Great Britain, mean-while, came away reassured that Canada remained safe from U.S. territorial ambitions. The only real losers of the War of 1812 were the Native Americans. They had fought heroically alongside the soldiers of Great Britain, all with the under-standing that they would be compensated with title to their ancestral lands. But under the terms of the Treaty of Ghent, Great Britain turned its back on its former allies. Instead of making good on its promises, Great Britain hid behind language contrived to deprive the Native Americans of what was theirs. According to the Treaty of Ghent, the Native Americans would be given "all the rights and privileges they enjoyed before the war," which were basically nonexistent.

"I pray this war puts us—in perception if not in reality—on an equal footing with the powers of Europe," Madison wrote. He continued:

> It will give meaning to the American blood spilled if, after all this, the royals and republicans of the old continent rec-ognize us as a force to be contemplated and calculated: an authority not to be ignored. I pray, for my own good, for this result—for some positive impact. Otherwise I rue the day when I shall go to my maker and have to look him in the eye. There must be meaning to the many graves: the graves in the ground and the graves in the wide and anonymous sea. Without this, we have not one thing at all. Without this, we have sinned in a terrible way.

The Makings
of a President

James Monroe, the fifth president of the United States, would do more than any chief executive before him to shape and influence American multinational diplomacy for succeeding generations of presidents and diplomats. Like Washington, Jefferson, and Madison before him, Monroe came from Virginia's planter society and entered office with indisputable credentials as a patriot and statesman.

EARLY LIFE OF JAMES MONROE

"He is tall and well formed," a female contemporary of James Monroe's wrote after meeting him at a White House reception. "His dress plain and in the old style. . . . His manner is quiet and dignified. From the frank, honest expression of his eye . . . I think he well deserves the encomium [high praise] passed upon him by the great Jefferson, who said, 'Monroe was so honest that if you turned his soul inside out there would not be a spot on it.'"

James Monroe was born on April 28, 1758, in Westmoreland County, Virginia. His father, Spence Monroe, was a prosperous planter who supplied young James with the advantages of education and opportunity. The Monroe family, meanwhile, boasted a very proud genealogy—one of the most respected lineages in all the colonies. Monroe's father, Spence, could trace his ancestors all the way back to a royal personage: King Edward III of England. Monroe's mother—Elizabeth Jones Monroe—was of Welsh extraction. Unlike most other women of her day, she was highly educated and well read, and inspired in her son a love of books and history. Early in his young life, James studied at Campbelton Academy—one of the most elite prep schools in Virginia. Another student at the same school was John Marshall, future chief justice of the U.S. Supreme Court. Monroe and Marshall rivaled each other in math, Latin, and other subjects.

Monroe's father died when the boy was 16. That same year, 1774, Monroe enrolled in Virginia's College of William and Mary, where he was soon distracted from his studies by the fervor of revolutionary politics. During the autumn of his freshman year, Monroe and several classmates made a clandestine midnight raid on the arsenal at the British Governor's Palace near the college. The students came away with 200 muskets and 300 swords—all of which eventually ended up in the hands of the revolutionary Virginia militia. Eventually, in 1775, Monroe dropped out of school altogether. Trading his textbooks for a rifle, he enlisted in the Williamsburg Militia and eventually the Continental Army (Third Virginia Regiment). Monroe enjoyed a superb career throughout the American Revolution, eventually rising in rank from lieutenant to lieutenant colonel.

During August 1776, Monroe's regiment found itself ordered northward to Harlem Heights, just above New York

City. Arriving during the American retreat from Manhattan Island, Monroe's contingent fought at the battles of Harlem Heights and White Plains. From there, Monroe's regiment traveled with Washington's retreating army through New Jersey and on to Pennsylvania. On December 26, 1776, at the Battle of Trenton, Monroe found himself in command of his regiment when his captain was wounded. Then it was his turn. "Soon after, I was shot through by a ball which grazed my breast."

After Monroe recovered from this relatively minor wound, he lobbied for and received appointment as the personal assistant to Major General William Alexander (Lord Stirling). Thereafter, Monroe participated in the battles of Brandywine and Germantown (1777), and in June 1778, he distinguished himself in the Battle of Monmouth, New Jersey.

Monroe left the Northern Army—stuck just outside New York City with no promise of action in the near future—in early 1779, with the intention of rejoining military forces closer to his Virginia home. Monroe arrived in Virginia that May and presented himself to the Virginia legislature, requesting a commission to lead a local militia. He came armed with a pistol, a sword, and a bayonet rifle. He also bore with him letters of recommendation from several major revolutionary leaders. General Washington, for one, said of Monroe: "He has in every instance maintained the reputation of a brave, active, and sensible officer." The Virginia legislature responded by commissioning him as a lieutenant colonel. However, Monroe's militia was never formed. Monroe saw no more direct military action during the American Revolution and from then on had to content himself with being an armchair soldier.

During the summer of 1779, Monroe was taken on as an aide and assistant by Thomas Jefferson, then governor of Virginia. Simultaneously, he became Jefferson's apprentice and student in the practice of law; this study eventually opening up a whole new world of ideas and possibilities for the young man: a life in politics and public service. As he later wrote Jefferson, at a time when his "plan of life" was "perplexed . . . you became acquainted with me and undertook the direction of my studies . . . my plan of life is now fixed." Jefferson and Monroe were to remain friends and allies for life.

POLITICIAN AND DIPLOMAT

From 1783 through 1786, Monroe served as a member of the Continental Congress, then meeting in New York City. It was during his time in New York that he met his future wife, Elizabeth Kortright, the daughter of a prominent Manhattan merchant. She was 10 years his junior. They married when he was 27 and she 17, and eventually moved to Fredericksburg, Virginia, where Monroe took up the practice of law.

During 1787, Monroe began serving in the Virginia Assembly. The following year he played a key role as a delegate to the Virginia Convention chosen to consider ratification of the newly drafted U.S. Constitution. As a young politician under the Jeffersonian spell, Monroe quite naturally joined the anti-Federalists (Jefferson's evolving Democratic-Republicans) in voting against ratification of the Constitution in its current draft. Like his fellow Jeffersonians, Monroe wanted changes that would allow the direct election of presidents and senators, and for the inclusion of a bill of rights. Partly due to arguments made by Monroe in the Virginia Convention regarding the omission of constitutional guarantees of key rights, the so-called "Bill of Rights" eventually became the first 10 amendments to the Constitution.

Monroe narrowly lost a congressional election to James Madison in 1790, but the Virginia state legislature appointed him to the U.S. Senate that same year. As a member of the Senate, he quickly and completely joined forces with James Madison and Thomas Jefferson against the Federalist lobby led

The most important foreign policy development during President Thomas Jefferson's first term was the purchase of the Louisiana Territory from France. The United States acquired the vast territory (828,000 square miles, or 2,144,520 square kilometers) for just $15 million. Depicted here are the signatories of the purchase, from left to right: French diplomat François Barbé-Marbois, U.S. Minister to France Robert R. Livingston, and James Monroe.

by Vice President John Adams and Secretary of the Treasury Alexander Hamilton.

In 1794, four years after his appointment to the Senate, Monroe accepted appointment from President Washington as minister to France. His time in Paris was to be short, however. Washington recalled Monroe two years later, after Monroe failed to publicly defend the Jay Treaty with Great Britain, with which he personally disagreed. During 1799, Monroe succeeded in being elected governor of Virginia, an office he was to hold for three one-year terms. Following this, during 1803, President Thomas Jefferson ordered Monroe back to Paris to help negotiate the purchase of the Louisiana Territory. After that, Monroe continued to work to advance the interests of the United States in Europe. Monroe represented the United States as minister to Great Britain between the years 1803 and 1807, interrupting this assignment only briefly with several months spent as special envoy to Spain during 1805.

Once Monroe returned home, dissident Democratic-Republicans induced him to challenge James Madison for the Democratic-Republican presidential nod in 1808. However, neither Monroe nor the electorate took the opportunity seriously. Monroe ran a halfhearted campaign, and Madison won the election with a wide margin. After being elected governor of Virginia yet again in January 1811, Monroe served only a few months before heading back to Washington the following April to take up duties as Madison's secretary of state. As the chief foreign service officer of the United States, Monroe at first endeavored strenuously to avoid the war with Great Britain, but soon agreed with the majority that arms must be taken up.

After the British landed in Maryland in 1814, Monroe personally led a team of scouts to observe their activities, and it was he who correctly determined that the British were headed for the city of Washington. Thereafter, Monroe himself personally ordered all essential documents removed from Washington in preparation for the British invasion. Following the eventual

British retreat from Washington, President Madison appointed Monroe secretary of war without asking him to step down from the job of secretary of state. Thus, Monroe held both positions during the latter stages of the War of 1812.

MONROE'S KEY ROLE WITH REGARD TO THE LOUISIANA PURCHASE

During January 1803, President Thomas Jefferson recommended that Monroe serve as special envoy to Robert R. Livingston, U.S. minister to France. As has been noted already, Monroe was a close political ally and friend of Jefferson's—a man whom Jefferson knew he could trust. In addition, Monroe also had a vested interest in the outcome of the Louisiana negotiations. He owned land in Kentucky, which at that time extended west as far as the lands of the French territory, and was known to believe in the idea of manifest destiny, the philosophy that the United States was destined to expand across the continent. In asking Monroe to join Livingston in the negotiations, Jefferson insisted that Monroe had "the unlimited confidence of the administration and of the western people." To this, the president added: "All eyes, all hopes, are now fixed on you, for on the event of this mission depends the future destinies of this republic."

After Monroe had accepted the assignment, the president spoke glowingly of Monroe and his prospects to Kentucky governor James Garrad. Jefferson told Garrad that Monroe carried with him to Paris the authority to enter into "arrangements that may effectually secure our rights & interest in the Mississippi, and in the country eastward of that." Monroe's orders, drawn up by Secretary of State Madison and approved by Jefferson, authorized him to offer up to $10 million for the purchase of New Orleans and all or some of Florida. If the $10 million proved not enough to buy all of that, then Monroe had orders to acquire New Orleans, or, through any other means, to establish U.S. access to the Mississippi River and an adjacent saltwater port.

(continues on page 36)

In November 1820, James Monroe won reelection, defeating John
Quincy Adams by a margin of 231 to 1 in the Electoral College.
Less than four months later, on Monday, March 5, 1821, Monroe
delivered his second inaugural address. Due to the bitterly cold and
rainy weather, he took the oath of office inside the newly built Hall
of the House of Representatives. In his speech, Monroe laid the
groundwork for the Monroe Doctrine—which he would bring before
Congress less than three years later—by promoting his views of
America's role in world affairs:

> By a treaty with the British Government, bearing date on the
> 20th of October, 1818, the convention regulating the commerce
> between the United States and Great Britain, concluded on the 3d
> of July, 1815, which was about expiring, was revived and contin-
> ued for the term of ten years from the time of its expiration. By
> that treaty, also, the differences which had arisen under the trea-
> ty of Ghent respecting the right claimed by the United States for
> their citizens to take and cure fish on the coast of His Britannic
> Majesty's dominions in America, with other differences on impor-
> tant interests, were adjusted to the satisfaction of both parties.
> No agreement has yet been entered into respecting the com-
> merce between the United States and the British dominions in the
> West Indies and on this continent. The restraints imposed on that
> commerce by Great Britain, and reciprocated by the United States
> on a principle of defense, continue still in force.
>
> The negotiation with France for the regulation of the com-
> mercial relations between the two countries, which in the course
> of the last summer had been commenced at Paris, has since
> been transferred to this city, and will be pursued on the part of

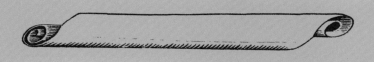

the United States in the spirit of conciliation, and with an earnest desire that it may terminate in an arrangement satisfactory to both parties.

Our relations with the Barbary Powers are preserved in the same state and by the same means that were employed when I came into this office. As early as 1801 it was found necessary to send a squadron into the Mediterranean for the protection of our commerce, and no period has intervened, a short term excepted, when it was thought advisable to withdraw it. The great interests which the United States have in the Pacific, in commerce and in the fisheries, have also made it necessary to maintain a naval force there. In disposing of this force in both instances the most effectual measures in our power have been taken, without interfering with its other duties, for the suppression of the slave trade and of piracy in the neighboring seas . . .

Europe is again unsettled and the prospect of war increasing. Should the flame light up in any quarter, how far it may extend it is impossible to foresee. It is our peculiar felicity to be altogether unconnected with the causes which produce this menacing aspect elsewhere. With every power we are in perfect amity, and it is our interest to remain so if it be practicable on just conditions. I see no reasonable cause to apprehend variance with any power, unless it proceed from a violation of our maritime rights. In these contests, should they occur, and to whatever extent they may be carried, we shall be neutral; but as a neutral power we have rights which it is our duty to maintain. . . . For more imminent dangers we should be prepared.

(continued from page 33)

Arriving in Paris on April 12, 1803, Monroe received a briefing from Livingston during which he was apprised of a significantly different, and better, offer placed on the table by the French. The news was good. Napoleon seemed disposed to liquidate virtually all of his holdings in North America, this due to stresses placed on his armed services in the maintenance of a large, extended empire. The army he had sent to Saint Domingue (present-day Haiti) to bring order after a rebellion by slaves had been virtually wiped out by an epidemic of yellow fever, and a new war between France and Great Britain seemed more than likely. Napoleon's minister of finance, François Barbé-Marbois, had always doubted Louisiana's economic value. According to Livingston, the finance minister had recently informed Napoleon that, in the event of war, the territory would most likely be seized by British troops sweeping down from Canada. The Louisiana terrain, in the French view, was too remote for France to defend adequately, and—as well—seemed hardly worth defending. Therefore, Napoleon expressed an interest in selling the entire Mississippi Valley and everything west of it to the United States. Monroe could hardly believe his good luck.

Seizing on this unique and wonderful opportunity before the French had a chance to change their minds, Monroe and Livingston immediately entered into negotiations with Foreign Minister Charles Maurice de Talleyrand-Périgord. Within two weeks, they had reached an agreement that far exceeded their authority to act, but which they presumed Jefferson would find attractive. What Livingston and Monroe arranged was the purchase of the entire Louisiana Territory, including New Orleans, for the price of $15 million. The total purchase added up to approximately 828,000 square miles. In fact, the transaction more than doubled the size of the United States at that time. Ironically, word of the purchase reached Jefferson just in time for him to announce it on an especially appropriate date: July 4, 1803.

PRESIDENT MONROE

James Monroe was inaugurated president on March 4, 1817. Unlike other presidents before him, Monroe took the oath of office at a temporary building then being used as a replacement for the U.S. Capitol, because the latter—after having been burned by the British in 1814—was still in the process of restoration. This "Brick Capitol" stood on the site currently occupied by the U.S. Supreme Court. Unlike previous presidents, Monroe recited the oath of office and delivered his inaugural speech outside rather than indoors. The move outside came at the suggestion of House Speaker Henry Clay, who thought the "Brick Capitol" to be too small and unkempt to house such an important ceremony. Thus, the whole proceeding took place on a large, temporary platform erected right next to the "Brick Capitol." The oath was administered by John Marshall, James Monroe's friend from boyhood, now chief justice of the United States.

"I should be destitute of feeling if I was not deeply affected by the strong proof which my fellow-citizens have given me of their confidence in calling me to the high office whose functions I am about to assume," Monroe began. He continued:

> As the expression of their good opinion of my conduct in the public service, I derive from it a gratification which those who are conscious of having done all that they could to merit it can alone feel. My sensibility is increased by a just estimate of the importance of the trust and of the nature and extent of its duties, with the proper discharge of which the highest interests of a great and free people are intimately connected. Conscious of my own deficiency, I cannot enter on these duties without great anxiety for the result. From a just responsibility I will never shrink, calculating with confidence that in my best efforts to promote the public welfare my motives will always be duly appreciated and my conduct be viewed with that candor and indulgence which I have experienced in other stations.

MONROE'S INAUGURATION

On March 4, 1817, James Monroe was inaugurated as the fifth president of the United States. Unlike previous presidents, Monroe took the oath of office and delivered his inaugural speech outdoors.

Later in his remarks, he spoke of his plan to build up U.S. forces to defend the country:

To secure us against these dangers our coast and inland frontiers should be fortified, our Army and Navy, regulated upon just principles as to the force of each, be kept in perfect order, and our militia be placed on the best practicable footing. To put our extensive coast in such a state of defense as to secure our cities and interior from invasion will be attended with expense, but the work when finished will be permanent, and it is fair to presume that a single campaign of invasion by a naval force superior to our own, aided by a few thousand land troops, would expose us to greater expense, without taking into the estimate the loss of property and distress of our citizens, than would be sufficient for this great work. Our land and naval forces should be moderate, but adequate to the necessary purposes—the former to garrison and preserve our fortifications and to meet the first invasions of a foreign foe, and, while constituting the elements of a greater force, to preserve the science as well as all the necessary implements of war in a state to be brought into activity in the event of war; the latter, retained within the limits proper in a state of peace, might aid in maintaining the neutrality of the United States with dignity in the wars of other powers and in saving the property of their citizens from spoliation. In time of war, with the enlargement of which the great naval resources of the country render it susceptible, and which should be duly fostered in time of peace, it would contribute essentially, both as an auxiliary of defense and as a powerful engine of annoyance, to diminish the calamities of war and to bring the war to a speedy and honorable termination.

Portrait of a Diplomat

James Monroe had played key diplomatic roles in previous administrations as both an emissary to foreign nations and as secretary of state. Now he employed another up-and-comer as his secretary of state—John Quincy Adams (1767–1848), most recently the ambassador to Great Britain and destined to succeed Monroe as president.

Adams arrived in Washington to assume his new duties in late September 1817. On the twentieth, he made his first formal call on Monroe. "The President, James Monroe," Adams wrote in his diary, "returned last Wednesday from a tour of nearly four months to the eastern and western parts of the United States. He is in the President's House, which is so far restored from the effects of the British visit in 1814 that it is now for the first time again habitable. But he is apprehensive of the effects of the fresh painting and plastering, and very desirous of visiting his family at his seat in Virginia. He is therefore going again to leave the city in two or three days, but said his absence would only be for a short time. He told me that Mr. [Richard] Rush would be my successor at the Court of Great Britain, and directed me to make out instructions for him."

Two days later, Adams was sworn in. "Mr. Rush called upon me this morning immediately after breakfast," he wrote in his diary, "and accompanied me to the office of the department of State, where the official oath, faithfully to execute the trust committed to me, prescribed by the Act of Congress establishing the Department of Foreign Affairs, and the oath to support the Constitution of the United States, were administered to me by Robert Brent, a justice of the peace for the District of Columbia."

A HERITAGE OF DIPLOMACY

Before John Quincy Adams became a diplomat, he spent long years watching his father, John Adams (1735–1826), in the same position. John Adams traveled to Europe in late 1780, accompanied by his two eldest sons, John Quincy (13) and Charles (10). Adams was to be abroad for many years, and his wife, Abigail, would not follow him until 1784.

One of the senior Adams's tasks while abroad was to serve as a joint commissioner (with Ben Franklin, John Jay, Henry Laurens, and Thomas Jefferson) to negotiate the treaty with Great Britain formally ending the American Revolution. During 1782, in negotiations at the Hague, the seat of government for the Netherlands, Adams secured the Netherlands' recognition of the United States. That same year he contracted the first of four loans from Amsterdam bankers to provide vital financial liquidity for the United States, and signed a detailed treaty of amity and commerce with the Dutch. One year later, in September 1783, after many months of intense negotiation, Adams and his fellow commissioners finally signed the Treaty of Paris with Great Britain. Then, from 1785 to 1788, John Adams—now accompanied by Abigail—served as the first

American minister to the Court of St. James's, the royal court of the United Kingdom, in London.

Adams's time as American minister in London was not particularly happy or productive. He, the rebel, felt unwelcome and uncomfortable in the British capital city. "Moreover," writes James Truslow Adams, "the country he represented was at that time in a rather despicable state. Congress was at its lowest ebb in mind, ability, and character, and the Union was in almost daily danger of disruption. When Adams attempted to insist upon the English carrying out the terms of the treaty, he was met by the query as to why the Americans did not do so on their part, to which there was little to answer."

Adams's initial presentation to King George was awkward. Neither man enjoyed the occasion. Each went stiffly through the motions of diplomatic protocol. In turn, British politicians treated Adams as though he represented an absurdity rather than a state. More than one insinuated that he was the ambassador of a country that was about to come apart at the seams. Many from the ranks of the British military and political elite made it clear to him that England's sword, though temporarily sheathed, could come out again at any moment. Through all of this, Adams himself remained quite grim and moody.

A letter written by Jefferson after spending much time with Adams in Great Britain says much about the tangled love-hate complexity that defined their friendship. Jefferson wrote to his fellow Virginian James Madison:

> You know the opinion I *formerly* entertained of *my friend* Mr. Adams. Yourself and the governor were the first who *shook* that opinion. I afterwards saw proofs which *convicted* him of a degree of *vanity* and of *blindness* to it, of which no germ *had appeared* in Congress. A *7-months'* intimacy with him here and as many *weeks* in *London* have given me opportunities of studying him closely. *He is vain, irritable and a bad calculator* of the force and

After narrowly defeating Thomas Jefferson in the 1796 election, John Adams (depicted here) became the second president of the United States. Like Washington, Adams was in favor of avoiding conflict with foreign powers.

probable effect of the motives which govern men. This is *all* the *ill* which can be *said of him*. He is as disinterested as the Being which made him: he is profound in his views, and accurate in his judgment *except where knowledge of the world* is necessary to form a judgment. He is so amiable that I pronounce you will love him if ever you become acquainted with him.

In short, the senior Adams was dogmatic, decided, and emphatic: quite sure of himself and his assumptions. The same could be said of Jefferson. Therein lay their problem. In their habits they were too alike not to attract, while at the same time clashing.

After eight years abroad, the elder Adams finally returned to the United States in 1788.

ENFANT TERRIBLE

John Quincy Adams was a person who was precocious from his earliest days and never changed. The second child and eldest son of John and Abigail Adams, John Quincy was born on July 11, 1767. As a boy during the American Revolution, young John Quincy watched the Battle of Bunker Hill from the top of Penn's Hill just above the old Adams family farm in Braintree, Massachusetts. Later on, as has been noted, John Quincy accompanied his father on early diplomatic missions to Europe. During the American Revolution, John Quincy attended school at a private academy outside Paris, the Latin School of Amsterdam, and Leiden University. As a young man of 14 and 15 years of age, he spent the years 1781 and 1782 in St. Petersburg, Russia, as private secretary and interpreter for Francis Dana, U.S. minister to the tsar's court. John Quincy subsequently assisted his father on various diplomatic missions throughout Europe.

While overseas, John Quincy developed an affinity for the Greek and Roman classics. Upon his return to the United

States in 1785, Harvard College granted him admission with advanced standing based on his studies at Leiden University. He graduated from Harvard in 1787. Thereafter, he studied law for three years with Theophilus Parsons in Newburyport, Massachusetts, and then went on to practice law in Boston, a pursuit that quickly bored him.

John Quincy next flirted with the life of a scholar and commentator. During the early 1790s, he developed a reputation as an orator and newspaper essayist. It was in this period that he composed the well-received "Letters of Publicola," which were written in response to Thomas Jefferson's approval of Thomas Paine's *Rights of Man*. (A decade later, simultaneous with a portion of his abbreviated term as U.S. Senator from Massachusetts, John Quincy would again become something of a scholar, serving as Boylston Professor of Rhetoric and Oratory at Harvard, from 1805 to 1809. Going forward, during all the unhappiest moments in his public career as a diplomat and politician, he would nearly always yearn loudly for Harvard, and the contentment he had found there.)

The 27-year-old Adams was completely satisfied with the life and work he had carved for himself as writer and commentator when, in 1794, everything changed. An appointment from President George Washington (combined with a large dose of parental goading) triggered the launch of John Quincy's diplomatic career. Washington appointed John Quincy—whose father at that time served as vice president—American minister to the Hague, in the Netherlands. Later on, during his father's presidency, John Quincy served from 1797 to 1801 as envoy to Prussia, stationed in Berlin, an appointment that drew charges of nepotism from Jefferson and other Democratic-Republicans.

Just as he was about to begin his work in Berlin, John Quincy stopped briefly in London, where he married Louisa Catherine Johnson—the daughter of the U.S. consul—on

(continues on page 48)

JOHN QUINCY ADAMS'S SPEECH ON DECEMBER 5, 1826

On July 4, 1821, while serving as U.S. secretary of state, John Quincy Adams delivered a speech in which he praised the virtues of American independence and the nation's relationship with European and South American countries. Adams was elected president in 1824, and over the coming years, he placed an emphasis on international relations. During his second annual message to Congress, on December 5, 1826, he discussed the U.S. military and expanded on his vision of international relations brought forth in his 1821 speech:

> It were, indeed, a vain and dangerous illusion to believe that in the present or probable condition of human society a commerce so extensive and so rich as ours could exist and be pursued in safety without the continual support of a military marine—the only arm by which the power of this Confederacy can be estimated or felt by foreign nations, and the only standing military force which can never be dangerous to our own liberties at home. A permanent naval peace establishment, therefore, adapted to our present condition, and adaptable to that gigantic growth with which the nation is advancing in its career, is among the subjects which have already occupied the foresight of the last Congress, and which will deserve your serious deliberations. Our Navy, commenced at an early period of our present political organization upon a scale commensurate with the incipient energies, the scanty resources, and the comparative indigence of our infancy, was even then found adequate to cope with all the powers of Barbary, save the first, and with one of the principle maritime powers of Europe. . . .
>
> The spirit of improvement is abroad upon the earth. It stimulates the hearts and sharpens the faculties not of our

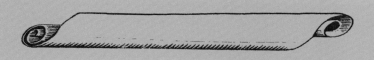

fellow citizens alone, but of the nations of Europe and of their rulers. While dwelling with pleasing satisfaction upon the superior excellence of our political institutions, let us not be unmindful that liberty is power; that the nation blessed with the largest portion of liberty must in proportion to its numbers be the most powerful nation upon earth, and that the tenure of power by man is, in the moral purposes of his Creator, upon condition that it shall be exercised to ends of beneficence, to improve the condition of himself and his fellow men.

While foreign nations less blessed with that freedom which is power than ourselves are advancing with gigantic strides in the career of public improvement, were we to slumber in indolence or fold up our arms and proclaim to the world that we are palsied by the will of our constituents, would it not be to cast away the bounties of Providence and doom ourselves to perpetual inferiority? In the course of the year now drawing to its close we have beheld . . . a new university unfolding its portals to the sons of science and holding up the torch of human improvement to eyes that seek the light. We have seen under the persevering and enlightened enterprise of another State the waters of our Western lakes mingle with those of the ocean. If undertakings like these have been accomplished in the compass of a few years by the authority of single members of our Confederation, can we, the representative authorities of the whole Union, fall behind our fellow servants in the exercise of the trust committed to us for the benefit of our common sovereign by the accomplishment of works important to the whole and to which neither the authority nor the resources of any one State can be adequate?

(continued from page 45)
July 26, 1797. He had met her in that city two years before. Her uncle Thomas Johnson, from Maryland, had—like John Quincy's father—been a signer of the Declaration of Independence. "At nine this morning I went," he wrote in his diary, "accompanied by my brother, to Mr. Johnson's and thence to the Church of the parish of All Hallows, Barking, where I was married to Louisa Catherine Johnson, the second daughter of Joshua and Catherine Johnson, by Mr. Hewlett. Mr. Johnson's family, Mr. Brooks, my brother, and Mr. J. Hall were present. We were married before eleven in the morning, and immediately after went out to see Tilney House, one of the splendid country seats for which this country is distinguished."

Although their marriage would often be troubled, it would nevertheless endure until John Quincy's death in 1848. The couple were to have four children: George Washington Adams (1801–1829), John Adams (1803–1834), Charles Francis Adams (1807–1886), and Louisa Catherine Adams (1811–1812).

PRINCIPLE PERSONIFIED

John Quincy was an extremely complex and eminently thoughtful individual who dwelled nearly constantly on serious matters, gave no quarter to lazy or shabby thinking, and held himself up to the very highest personal standards of logic and reason. His intensity and focus made him at times seem quite isolated from the people surrounding him. Even his own son Charles once described him as "impenetrable." Never at rest intellectually, morally, or ethically, he sometimes lapsed into depths of depression. The one principle that drove him was duty, and the one pleasure that satisfied his nervous energy was the constant intellectual pursuit of new avenues of study. In his spare time, he investigated and pursued gardening, swimming, astronomy, and religion with equal passion.

In terms of religion, he started out, despite his parents' liberality in these matters, a strict Calvinist conservative.

JOHN QUINCY ADAMS.

JOHN QUINCY ADAMS
MASSACHUSETTS

John Adams's eldest son, John Quincy, believed in protecting the United States' sovereignty in the Americas. His belief in equality for all nations led to his drafting of the Monroe Doctrine, which would serve as the basis of U.S. foreign policy.

He eventually joined his parents in the liberal wing of New England Congregationalism. Thus, John Quincy, following the trail blazed by his church, evolved during the second decade of the nineteenth century into a Unitarian, though not an overly dogmatic one. Throughout his life, he would profess to feel at home in virtually any Christian church. In fact, he would often attend two services on Sunday: one Unitarian, the other Episcopal. But always, in all things—in religion and in politics—he remained true, first and foremost, to his own principles and to his own view of what was right.

John Quincy Adams's contrariness extended to politics. During the first decade of the nineteenth century, while serving as a young, first-term senator from Massachusetts, John Quincy renounced his father's Federalist Party and supported Thomas Jefferson's embargo of 1807: a move with which many Massachusetts voters, including his father, stridently disagreed. His principles extended to foreign policy, where he formulated and practiced a philosophy he convincingly articulated in a brief speech before the House of Representatives on July 4, 1821. "What has America done for the benefit of mankind?" Adams asked his listeners. He continued:

> Let our answer be this: America, with the same voice which spoke herself into existence as a nation, proclaimed to mankind the inextinguishable rights of human nature, and the only lawful foundations of government. America, in the assembly of nations, since her admission among them, has invariably, though often fruitlessly, held forth to them the hand of honest friendship, of equal freedom, of generous reciprocity. She has uniformly spoken among them, though often to heedless and often to disdainful ears, the language of equal liberty, of equal justice, and of equal rights. She has, in the lapse of nearly half a century, without a single exception, respected the independence of other nations while asserting and maintaining her own. She has abstained from interference in the concerns of others, even when conflict has been for principles to which she clings, as to the last vital drop that visits the heart. She has seen that probably for centuries

to come, all the contests of . . . the European world, will be contests of inveterate power, and emerging right. Wherever the standard of freedom and Independence has been or shall be unfurled, there will her heart, her benedictions and her prayers be. But she goes not abroad, in search of monsters to destroy. She is the well-wisher to the freedom and independence of all. She is the champion and vindicator only of her own. She will commend the general cause by the countenance of her voice, and the benignant sympathy of her example. She well knows that by once enlisting under other banners than her own, were they even the banners of foreign independence, she would involve herself beyond the power of extrication, in all the wars of interest and intrigue, of individual avarice, envy, and ambition, which assume the colors and usurp the standard of freedom. . . . [America's] glory is not dominion, but liberty. Her march is the march of the mind. She has a spear and a shield: but the motto upon her shield is, Freedom, Independence, Peace. This has been her Declaration: this has been, as far as her necessary intercourse with the rest of mankind would permit, her practice.

Early Diplomacy in Monroe's First Term

The main diplomatic accomplishments of President James Monroe and his secretary of state, John Quincy Adams, between the years 1817 and 1821 involved the overcoming of key dangers of the United States' key competitors for influence and territory on the North American continent: Great Britain and Spain.

THE TREATY OF 1818

John Quincy Adams's first order of business as secretary of state was dealing with tricky issues between Great Britain and the United States that had been left unresolved by the Treaty of Ghent. With the assistance of the new minister to Great Britain, Richard Rush, John Quincy negotiated a new agreement—signed in 1818—that established the northwest boundary between the United States and Canada at the 49th parallel

As secretary of state, John Quincy Adams was instrumental in helping to negotiate the Treaty of Ghent (depicted here). The agreement, signed in 1814, officially ended the War of 1812, but left many issues unresolved, including the establishment of a northwest boundary between the United States and Canada.

to the Rocky Mountains, leaving the terrain beyond open to settlement by citizens of either nation. Of equal importance, the Treaty of 1818 also reaffirmed American fishing rights off the coasts of Newfoundland and Labrador. Additionally, it reaffirmed previously articulated commercial understandings between the two powers, while agreeing to leave for further arbitration the claims of slaveholders for "property" seized by the British during the War of 1812.

COMPLICATIONS IN FLORIDA

One of the key hindrances standing in the way of good relations between Spain and the United States was Spanish territorial claims in eastern Florida. (Western Florida had been part of the United States since 1813.) To complicate matters, Adams and Monroe suspected that the Spanish—from their eastern Florida base, and with subtle encouragement from Great Britain—had been arming Seminole tribesmen and encouraging their incursions into southern Georgia. It was because of this that, in March 1818, General Andrew Jackson led his troops into Spanish Florida, seized the Spanish bastion at Pensacola, and, in late April, put to death two British traders suspected of inspiring the Seminole tribesmen to their crimes—an action roundly condemned by Luis de Onís y Gonzales, Spain's minister to the United States.

In June, the topic of General Jackson's actions in Florida dominated a cabinet meeting. "The President and all the members of the Cabinet, except myself, are of opinion that Jackson acted not only without, but against, his instructions: that he has committed war upon Spain, which cannot be justified, and in which, if not disavowed by the Administration, they will be abandoned by the country," wrote Adams. He continued:

> My opinion is that there was no real, though an apparent, violation of his instructions: that his proceedings were justified by the necessity of the case, and by the misconduct of the Spanish officers in Florida. The question is embarrassing and complicated, not only as involving that of an actual war with Spain, but that of the Executive power to authorize hostilities without a declaration of war by Congress. There is no doubt that defensive acts of hostility may be authorized by the Executive; but Jackson was authorized to cross the Spanish line in pursuit of the Indian enemy. . . . Calhoun, the Secretary of War, generally of sound, judicious, and comprehensive mind, seems in this case to be personally offended with the idea that Jackson has set at nought the instructions of the Department. The President supposes there might be cases which would have justified Jackson's measures, but that he has not made out his case.

The next morning, at another cabinet meeting, the debate continued. Adams wrote,

> Second Cabinet meeting at the President's, and the question of the course to be pursued with relation to General Jackson's proceedings in Florida recurred. As the opinion is unanimously against Jackson excepting mine, my range of argument now is only upon the degree to which his acts are to be disavowed. It was urged that the public dissatisfaction at the taking of Pensacola is so great that the Administration must immediately and publicly disclaim having given any authority for it, and publish all the instructions given to him [Jackson] to throw the blame entirely upon him.

Again, on June 17, the topic remained Jackson:

> Cabinet meeting at the President's—the discussion continued upon the answer to be given to Onis, and the restoration of Florida to Spain. The weakness and palsy of my right hand make it impossible for me to report this discussion, in which I continued to oppose the unanimous opinions of the President, the Secretary of the Treasury Crawford, the Secretary of War Calhoun, and the Attorney General Wirt. I have thought that the whole conduct of General Jackson was justifiable under his orders, although he certainly had none to take any Spanish fort. My principle is that everything he did was defensive: that as such it was neither war against Spain nor violation of the Constitution.

Once more, on June 21, the subject of Jackson and the Florida incursion arose. "A Cabinet meting, at which the second draft of my letter to Mr. Onís was read and finally fixed," Adams recorded. He continued:

> Mr. Wirt read what he called a second edition of his article for the *National Intelligencer*. I strenuously re-urged my

objections, especially to a paragraph declaring that the President thought he had no constitutional power to have authorized General Jackson to take Pensacola. . . . I finally gave up
the debate, acquiescing in the determination which had been
taken. The Administration were placed in a dilemma from
which it is impossible for them to escape censure by some,
and factious crimination by many. If they avow and approve
Jackson's conduct, they incur the double responsibility of
having commenced a war against Spain, and of warring
in violation of the Constitution without the authority of
Congress. If they disavow him, they must give offence to all
his friends, encounter the shock of his popularity, and have
the appearance of truckling to Spain. For all this I should be
prepared. But the mischief of this determination lies deeper:
1. It is weakness, and confession of weakness. 2. The disclaimer
of power in the Executive is of dangerous example and of evil
consequences. 3. There is injustice to the officer in disavowing
him, when in principle he is strictly justifiable. . . .

Calhoun says he has heard that the court-martial at first
acquitted the two Englishmen, but that Jackson sent the
case back to them. He says, also, that last winter there was a
company formed in Tennessee, who sent Jackson's nephew
to Pensacola and purchased Florida lands, and that Jackson
himself is reported to be interested in the speculation. I
hope not.

THE TRANSCONTINENTAL TREATY OF 1819

Both Monroe and Adams realized Spain had its hands full controlling and maintaining its many colonies in Latin America,
and that Florida—presenting no genuine strategic advantage
for the Spanish—was probably the most disposable of all Spanish possessions worldwide. On July 10, 1818—shortly after the
Jackson flap—Adams received confirmation of this suspicion
from the French ambassador to the United States.

"Had an interview at the office with Hyde de Neuville, the
French Minister," Adams wrote in his diary,

all upon our affairs with Spain. He says that Spain will cede the Floridas to the United States, and let the lands go for the indemnities due to our citizens, and he urged that we should take the Sabine for the western boundary, which I told him was impossible. He urged this subject very strenuously for more than an hour. As to Onis's note of invective against General Jackson, which I told him as a good friend to Onis he should advise him to take back, he said I need not answer it for a month or two, perhaps not at all, if in the meantime we could come to an arrangement of the other differences.

In the end, Adams waited for the dust to settle over the Florida raid before pursing Onís and endeavoring to shape the type of treaty suggested by the French. Through diligent talks with Onís conducted between February 12 and 20, 1819, Adams eventually secured such an agreement. This document is sometimes known as the Adams-Onís Treaty. The two men met over the course of a week, face-to-face, in the end creating a historic treaty that pushed aside many of the barriers that had previously stood in the path of the United States as it sought recognition as a continental power.

Adams negotiated purchase of eastern Florida for the price of $5 million, a figure to be paid not to Spain, but rather to Americans with claims against Spain. Adams also obtained an excellent and generous boundary between the Louisiana Purchase lands and Spanish Texas. This newly articulated line ran along the Sabine, Red, and Arkansas rivers to the Continental Divide, where it turned west as far as the Pacific Ocean along the 42nd parallel. In addition, Spain agreed to renounce any claim to Oregon.

Adams wrote in his diary on February 22:

Mr. Onis came at eleven with Mr. Stoughton, one of the persons attached to his Legation. The two copies of the treaty made out at his house were ready: none of ours were entirely finished. We exchanged the original full powers on

GENERAL ANDREW JACKSON.
The Hero, the Sage and the Patriot.

In 1817, President James Monroe sent General Andrew Jackson into what is today Alabama and southern Georgia to defend U.S. settlers from attacks by the Seminole Indians. Jackson, however, continued into Florida and captured the Spanish fort at Pensacola. Although officially condemned by President Monroe, Jackson's actions gave the United States an excuse to annex Florida.

both sides, which I believe to be the correct course on the conclusion of treaties, though at Ghent, and on the conclusion of the Convention of 3rd July 1815, the originals were only exhibited and copies exchanged. I had one of the copies of the treaty, and Mr. Onis the other. I read the English side, which he collated, and he the Spanish side, which I collated. We then signed and sealed both copies on both sides—I first on the English and he first on the Spanish side. . . .

The acquisition of the Floridas has long been an object of earnest desire to this country. The acknowledgment of a definite line of boundary to the South Sea forms a great epoch in our history. The first proposal of it in this negotiation was my own, and I trust it is now secured beyond the reach of revocation. It was not even among our claims by the Treaty of Independence with Great Britain. It was not among our pretensions under the purchase of Louisiana—for that gave us only the range of the Mississippi and its waters. I first introduced it in the written proposal of 31st October last, after having discussed it verbally both with Onis and De Neuville. It is the only peculiar and appropriate right acquired by this treaty in the event of its ratification.

All seemed well, until the treaty went to the House of Representatives. There, to Adams's utter horror, complications arose, and did so in the most humiliating manner. Henry Clay—a rival of Adams's who, like the secretary of state, had his eye on the Executive Mansion—discovered a serious flaw in the language of the treaty's Article VIII. With some apparent delight, Clay let both Monroe and Adams know that the document as drafted contained an enormous loophole allowing two large Spanish grants of Florida land to remain valid after the United States took possession.

Studying the issue, Adams was devastated to realize Clay was right. During his negotiations with Onís, Adams had

(continues on page 62)

KEY ARTICLES OF THE TRANSCONTINENTAL TREATY

The Transcontinental Treaty, also called the Adams-Onís Treaty of 1819, was an agreement between the United States and Spain that divided each country's North American claims. The boundary established by the two nations ran from the southeastern corner of present-day Louisiana, north and west to what is now Wyoming, and then west at 42°N latitude to the Pacific Ocean. Most importantly, Spain gave up Florida and Oregon Country in exchange for the right to hold onto what is today Texas and the American Southwest.

ARTICLE II
His Catholic Majesty cedes to the United States, in full property and sovereignty, all the territories which belong to him, situated to the eastward of the Mississippi, known by the name of East and West Florida. . . .

ARTICLE III
The boundary-line between the two countries, west of the Mississippi, shall begin on the Gulf of Mexico, at the mouth of the river Sabine, in the sea, continuing north, along the western bank of that river, to the 32d degree of latitude; thence, by a line due north, to the degree of latitude where it strikes the Rio Roxo of Nachitoches, or Red River; then following the course of the Rio Roxo westward, to the degree of longitude 100 west from London and 23 from Washington; then, crossing the said Red River, and running thence, by a line due north, to the river Arkansas; thence, following the course of the southern bank of the Arkansas, to its source, in latitude 42 north; and thence, by that parallel of latitude, to the South Sea. The whole being as laid down in Melish's map of the United States, published at Philadelphia, improved to the first of January, 1818. But if the source of the Arkansas River shall be

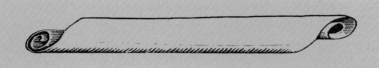

found to fall north or south of latitude 42, then the line shall run from the said source due south or north, as the case may be, till it meets the said parallel of latitude 42, and thence, along the said parallel, to the South Sea. . . .

The two high contracting parties agree to cede and renounce all their rights, claims, and pretensions to the territories described by the said line, that is to say: The United States hereby cede to His Catholic Majesty, and renounce forever, all their rights, claims, and pretensions, to the territories lying west and south of the above-described line; and, in like manner, His Catholic Majesty cedes to the said United States all his rights, claims, and pretensions to any territories east and north of the said line, and for himself, his heirs, and successors, renounces all claim to the said territories forever.

ARTICLE IV

To fix this line with more precision, and to place the landmarks which shall designate exactly the limits of both nations, each of the contracting parties shall appoint a Commissioner and a surveyor, who shall meet before the termination of one year from the date of the ratification of this treaty at Nachitoches, on the Red River, and proceed to run and mark the said line, from the mouth of the Sabine to the Red River, and from the Red River to the river Arkansas, and to ascertain the latitude of the source of the said river Arkansas, in conformity to what is above agreed upon and stipulated and the line of latitude 42, to the South Sea. . . .

ARTICLE V

The inhabitants of the ceded territories shall be secured in the free exercise of their religion, without any restriction. . . .

(continued from page 59)

persuaded Spain to accept the year 1802 as the deadline after which such grants would be rescinded. But the treaty as presented by the Spanish stipulated the much later year of 1818, and Adams had not caught it. The mistake was both an embarrassment and a potentially fatal eventuality with regards to the treaty. Monroe suspected international fraud. Adams told a friend how all along he had feared the treaty "was too great a blessing not to be followed shortly by something to alloy it." Nevertheless, Adams immediately moved to fix the situation, after having been, in his own words, purged "of all vanity and self-conceit."

Adams enlisted the aid of Jean-Guillaume Hyde Baron de Neuville (the French ambassador, and also a close personal friend) in encouraging Onís to revise the treaty, and send the revised draft to Madrid for approval. Thereafter, Adams—and the treaty—lingered in limbo for many months. Adams did not receive the approved treaty back until February 12, 1821. Nearly immediately, the Senate reapproved the document, the two nations formally exchanged ratifications, and the United States took full possession of the desired lands.

"If I never do another thing in this life," Adams wrote in a rare moment of self-satisfaction, "I shall feel my days have been worthwhile when I look back on the agreement just accomplished with Onis." He continued:

> The destiny of our country, the great western momentum that will most certainly be the stuff of our history, is now a certainty. We finally hold undisputed dominion over our Continent from one ocean to another: from the sunrise to the sunset. No amount of partisan scarping can diminish this achievement. No low blow of politics can smear it. The thing will stand over long decades, and no man can doubt its value. What we have wrought, we have wrought well. What we have mapped out is the landscape for a great democratic

communion. This is the bedrock upon which nationhood will be built: the foundation stone in the most real and tactile sense. When my grandchildren seek to wonder who I was and why I mattered, let them be pointed to the piece of paper I've signed with Onis. When God asks me what my contribution may have been to the betterment of this fragile world, let him be pointed to the same document.

Virtually every historian of early American diplomacy cites the Adams-Onís Treaty (sometimes referred to as the Transcontinental Treaty) as the hallmark achievement of Adams's first four years as secretary of state. At the time, it must have seemed that no other accomplishment would ever outshine the 1819 agreement with Spain. However, within four more short years, John Quincy Adams would play a key role in defining and enunciating something even more important. A philosophy that was to become a fundamental principle of U.S. foreign policy for succeeding generations and still influences international relations to this very day: the Monroe Doctrine.

The Disintegration of South America

In order to understand the rationale behind the formulation of the Monroe Doctrine, one must first understand the situation in South America at that time, which formed a vital backdrop to the environment in which John Quincy Adams and James Monroe did their work. During this period, Spain's dominion in the Americas was disintegrating, with the king in Madrid facing revolution in virtually all of his American colonies. Following the examples of the American and French revolutions, and with Spain distracted and weakened by the Napoleonic Wars, liberation movements gained strength in a range of South American colonies, including New Granada (Venezuela and Colombia), La Plata (Paraguay and Argentina), and Peru (Ecuador, Peru, Bolivia, and Chile).

Spain had all it could handle in attempting to manage its war with France up to 1813. After this, the Spanish government found itself weakened by civil wars that continued throughout the 1820s. In the midst of these stresses, the Spanish leaders could give little direction to their colonies. Thus, throughout South America, local power centers emerged to rule the various colonies. These were called then, as they are today, *juntas*. The first outright dictator to emerge and declare revolt was strongman José Gaspar Rodríguez de Francia, who seized control of Paraguay in 1814. King Ferdinand VII attempted to restore his authority by sending troops and ships. However, this action did not lead to immediate victory for Spain, but rather to civil war that soon extended throughout South America. Throughout the continent, colonies rose in rebellion against Ferdinand, with most working in concert with rebel armies led by Simón Bolívar (1783–1830) and José de San Martín (1778–1850).

BOLÍVAR IN VENEZUELA AND COLOMBIA

Born in Caracas, Venezuela, on July 24, 1783, Simón Bolívar came from a family that originally hailed from the Basque region of northern Spain. His immediate ancestors, however, had all been born in Venezuela. By Simón's generation, the family held a leading position among Venezuela's economic, cultural, and political elite.

Bolívar's father was Colonel Juan Vicente Bolívar y Ponte. His mother was Dona Concepción Palacios Blanco. The father died suddenly and tragically in January 1786, before the boy turned three. Thus Bolívar's education was largely overseen by his mother up until 1792, when she, too, passed away, leaving him an orphan, albeit a smart and precocious one.

At age 14, while continuing to be homeschooled by a monk named Francisco de Andujar, Bolívar joined a battalion in the Aragua Valley, a unit that had been headed by his father many years before. Within a year, at the green age of only 15, Bolívar received a promotion to the rank of second lieutenant. During his military training, Bolívar devoted his spare time to learning mathematics, topography, chemistry, physics, and, of course, the classics of history and literature.

Simón Bolívar, who is known in Spanish as "El Libertador," freed several South American countries from Spanish rule, including Venezuela, Colombia, and Bolivia, which is named in his honor. Bolívar is depicted in this 1859 painting by Venezuelan artist Arturo Michelena.

Early in 1799, Bolívar went to Spain. Living in Madrid, he immersed himself in higher-level studies. Like other young men from privileged families destined for the life of a gentleman, he combined the advanced study of essential subjects with more frivolous pursuits. Along with history, classical and modern literature, the sciences, mathematics, and French, Bolívar also studied fencing and dance. During his time in Madrid, he made the acquaintance of the beautiful Maria Teresa Rodriguez del Toro y Alayza. The two fell in love nearly immediately. They married on May 26, 1802, with several of Bolívar's Madrid friends in attendance. Not long after the wedding, Simón and his beloved traveled to Venezuela, where tragedy struck. Maria died the following January. Soon, the brokenhearted Bolívar returned to Europe. After brief stays in Cadiz and Madrid, he took up residence in Paris during the spring of 1804.

Paris proved the ideal city for Bolívar. First, the city was a center for European politics and diplomacy. World leaders came and went, and history seemed to be made on a daily basis. Secondly, it was populated with beautiful women, with whom he tried to heal the bitter wound of the loss of his wife. Every evening, Bolívar could be found at fancy balls and every day at sporting events. He gave much time to his social life, but an equal amount of time to his studies and to meeting the great minds to be found in the city some called "the capital of the World."

Bolívar also studied up on the great revolutions taking place across Europe and around the globe—the great wars of rebellion that promised to transform the world. Ultimately, he decided that he wished to play a role in that transformation—in the liberation of the world from colonial slavery. More precisely, Bolívar began to write and talk about what became the grand master strategy of his life: liberating his native South America from Spanish authority.

(continues on page 70)

SIMÓN BOLÍVAR'S
LETTER FROM JAMAICA

In 1810, Simón Bolívar led a group of revolutionaries in overthrowing the Spanish-led government in Venezuela. Unfortunately, Bolívar's group, in turn, was overthrown in 1814 and forced to flee to Jamaica. While in Jamaica, Bolívar wrote his famous "Letter from Jamaica," which he delivered on September 6, 1815. In this "letter," written in response to a Jamaican who empathized with his desire to liberate South America, Bolívar promoted Latin American unity and introduced his ideas for a republican government:

> The war-like state of the La Plata River provinces has purged that territory and led their victorious armies to Upper Perú, arousing Arequipa and worrying the royalists in Lima. Nearly one million inhabitants there now enjoy liberty.
>
> The territory of Chile, populated by 800,000 souls, is fighting the enemy who is seeking her subjugation; but to no avail, because those who long ago put an end to the conquests of this enemy, the free and indomitable Araucanians, are their neighbors and compatriots. Their sublime example is proof to those fighting in Chile that a people who love independence will eventually achieve it.
>
> The viceroyalty of Perú, whose population approaches a million and a half inhabitants, without doubt suffers the greatest subjection and is obliged to make the most sacrifices for the royal cause; and, although the thought of cooperating with that part of America may be vain, the fact remains that it is not tranquil, nor is it capable of restraining the torrent that threatens most of its provinces. . . .
>
> New Granada, which is, so to speak, the heart of America, obeys a general government, save for the territory of Quito which

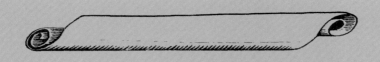

is held only with the greatest difficulty by its enemies, as it is strongly devoted to the country's cause; and the provinces of Panamá and Santa Marta endure, not without suffering, the tyranny of their masters. . . .

Europe could do Spain a service by dissuading her from her rash obstinacy, thereby at least sparing her the costs she is incurring and the blood she is expending. And if she will fix her attention on her own precincts she can build her prosperity and power upon more solid foundations than doubtful conquests, precarious commerce, and forceful exactions from remote and powerful peoples. Europe herself, as a matter of common sense policy, should have prepared and executed the project of American independence, not alone because the world balance of power so necessitated, but also because this is the legitimate and certain means through which Europe can acquire overseas commercial establishments. A Europe which is not moved by the violent passions of vengeance, ambition, and greed, as is Spain, would seem to be entitled, by all the rules of equity, to make clear to Spain where her best interests lie.

All of the writers who have treated this matter agree on this point. Consequently, we have had reason to hope that the civilized nations would hasten to our aid in order that we might achieve that which must prove to be advantageous to both hemispheres. How vain has been this hope! Not only the Europeans but even our brothers of the North have been apathetic bystanders in this struggle which, by its very essence, is the most just, and in its consequences the most noble and vital of any which have been raised in ancient or in modern times. Indeed, can the far-reaching effects of freedom for the hemisphere which Columbus discovered ever be calculated?

(continued from page 67)

During the final months of 1806, Simón Bolívar went home to Venezuela and began structuring the revolution that would finally come to a head in 1811. During the ensuing years, Simón and his men laid siege to the Spanish royalist forces with great success. It seemed history and public sentiment were on their side. During the years between 1817 and 1820, Bolívar liberated Venezuela and Colombia. In the midst of this, during the year 1819, Bolívar established the Republic of Gran Colombia (comprising territories of the modern-day countries of Colombia, Ecuador, Panama, and Venezuela) with himself as president. Bolívar subsequently led his amalgamated forces on a torturous trek through the Andes, at the end of which they defeated the Spanish in Ecuador.

SAN MARTÍN IN ARGENTINA, CHILE, AND PERU

Born February 25, 1778, José de San Martín was the fifth child of native Spaniards Juan de San Martín and Gregoria Matorras. San Martín first saw the light of the world in the town of Yapeyú, which was formerly a Jesuit mission station in Guaraní Indian territory, and at the time of his birth a part of the Viceroyalty of Río de la Plata, one of the four viceroyalties that Spain created during its colonization of Central and South America. Yapeyú was a beautiful place that stood near today's Paso de los Libres, in the Corrientes Province of Argentina. San Martín's father was a professional soldier. He was also the government administrator of Yapeyú.

During 1784, the six-year-old San Martín returned to Spain with his parents. There, his parents put him into an excellent school, Madrid's Real Seminario de Nobles, which he attended from 1785 through 1789. It was at this school that he formed the most vital and important friendship of his life. Bernardo O'Higgins, a child of mixed Irish-Spanish heritage from Chile, was San Martín's junior by several months. The two boys would one day make history together. Both, it seemed, were fixated on the liberation of their homelands from Spanish domination.

Returning to Argentina, San Martín fought his first battle against the Spanish in February 1813. During that month, he attacked and defeated royalist troops on the banks of the Rio Paraná at San Lorenzo. Shortly after this victory, San Martín went into northern Argentina with the idea of moving even farther north, into Peru, to destroy the viceroyalty that dominated the countryside. However, before he could make his move, he became ill. San Martín wound up quietly biding his time in northern Argentina for much of 1814, making his plans, and waiting for the opportune moment to strike. The longer he waited, the more formidable the task of crossing the Andes (over terrain that is today Bolivia) into Peru seemed to become.

It was at this fortuitous moment that San Martín found himself reunited with his school-chum friend from Madrid, Bernardo O'Higgins. The latter had been forced to flee Chile with royalist forces in pursuit following the embarrassing defeat at the Battle of Rancagua. O'Higgins was not alone. With him traveled literally thousands of earnest Chilean men bent on the liberation of not only their homeland, but all of South America.

For the next three years, San Martín collaborated with O'Higgins to develop strategy for a full-scale ground war of liberation. The army they built unified regiments of Chileans, Argentines, and others. Eventually, San Martín's excellence in strategy, his stirring leadership, and his bold vision for a united front against Spanish aggression would win him the title "Knight of the Andes."

At about this time, in 1816, San Martín took the initiative to gather, in Tucumán, Argentina, representatives from all the provinces of South America. There they formed the *Congreso de Tucumán.* During these meetings and talks, San Martín insisted on the necessity for total and complete independence from Spain, and the similar necessity for Spain's rule to be replaced by liberal-constitutional governments. The delegates of the conference agreed and passed a unified declaration of independence in July 1816.

During January 1817, San Martín and O'Higgins led their combined armies over a rigorous and grueling pass through the Andes Mountains, some 15,000 feet high, and into Chile. Thereafter, they met and crushed royalist forces on February 12 at Casas de Chacabuco and soon took Santiago. Another victory at Maipo, in north-central Chile, soon followed in April 1818, and this last battle secured Chile's independence. After this, revolutionary leaders asked San Martín to become supreme dictator of Chile. This he declined; however, he did take the title generalissimo of the United Army of the Andes and Chile. Following this, San Martín initiated discussions with royalist forces in Peru, trying to induce those troops to break from Spain and create a new, independent state. When all of San Martín's lobbying came to nothing, he turned to military action. San Martín assembled his ground troops one more time and added to their power the new Chilean Navy commanded by his friend O'Higgins. By the end of 1821, Lima had been taken and the royalists there had been made to surrender.

In the wake of his great victory, San Martín was named Protector del Peru and assumed powers as the head of the new Peruvian government. As leader, he immediately implemented wide-ranging social and political reforms such as instituting a free press, establishing a national library, and increasing government support for free, public education. The efforts made him even more popular among Peruvians than he had previously been, and helped him stave off a counteroffensive by soldiers loyal to the royalist cause.

BOLÍVAR AND SAN MARTÍN MEET

By early 1822, only two royalist armies still remained in South America. The first surrounded Quito, in Colombia, and the second occupied the rural southern portion of Peru. Early in the spring of 1822, Simón Bolívar sent troops from Colombia to overwhelm the royalists surrounding Quito. They met with

Much like Simón Bolívar, José de San Martín (depicted here with his staff) is celebrated as a hero by many Latin Americans. San Martín liberated Argentina, Chile, and Peru from Spanish control but relinquished his rule to Bolívar at the height of his power.

success in May. Bolívar arrived in Colombia that July and officially annexed the territory from Spain. At the same time, San Martín's combined Argentine, Chilean, and Peruvian forces attempted, without much early success, to quash the Spanish royalists south of Lima.

After several lackluster battles, San Martín turned to Bolívar for assistance. Uncharacteristically for a man of his massive ego, San Martín went so far as to offer himself as Bolívar's second in command in their shared fight to force Spain out of Peru and all of South America. After receiving word of this offer, Bolívar asked San Martín to come meet him at Guayaquil, Colombia (present-day Ecuador). Upon his arrival at Guayaquil on July 25, 1822, San Martín received a hero's welcome with parades, speeches, and salutes. Following this, he met behind closed doors with Bolívar for an hour or so. Then, without fanfare, he left Guayaquil and returned to Peru.

There are no written minutes of their discussions, but evidently the two men argued. Although they shared a dream of a South America free of Spanish royalist rule, they differed fundamentally on what the future should hold for that region, the modes of government to be established, and other key factors. In the midst of these talks, the two men—each larger than life—found that they did not care for one another personally. Most historians believe that Bolívar, in the course of his discussions with San Martín, announced that he would refuse to send his men into Peru while San Martín was there.

Upon his return to Peru, San Martín abdicated his rule. Shortly thereafter, he went to Chile and from there to retirement at his small farm in Mendoza, Argentina. Concurrent with these events, Bolívar's forces defeated the Spanish royalists at the battles of Junín and Ayacucho, thus completing the liberation of Peru.

THE NEW REPUBLICS

The United States was quick to recognize the new Latin American republics, exchanging ambassadors with Argentina, Chile, Peru, and Colombia in 1822. (Mexico was also independent of Spain by this time and formally recognized by the United States as a sovereign power.) At the same time, following the end of the Napoleonic Wars, Russia and France proposed that

Great Britain join them in helping Spain regain her New World colonies. (One year earlier, in 1822, the Congress of Verona met, which led to the intervention of European governments to restore absolute government in Spain, so a similar effort in South America seemed a logical move for those same powers.)

Although wedded to the idea of empire, and to the principle of monarchies, Great Britain nevertheless refused to become included, primarily for economic reasons. South America as a whole constituted, at the time, a much larger market for British goods than even the United States, and Great Britain preferred the idea of trade with distinct and disparate Latin American states rather than with a chain of linked colonies under Spanish dominion. The joint Russian/French overture, however, gave a strong hint as to the plans of other European powers vis-à-vis South America, and alerted the British as to what would come if steps were not taken to shore up the defensive alliances of the fledgling republics.

These strategic realities frame the events that led to the enunciation of the Monroe Doctrine in December 1823. Ironically, several years before this, James Monroe himself had thought of allying with the British to advance the cause of the Latin American revolutionaries. The following entry comes from John Quincy Adams's diary for July 25, 1818:

> The President two days ago very abruptly asked me to see Mr. Bagot and propose through him to the British Government an immediate cooperation between the United States and Great Britain to promote the independence of South America. I asked him what part of South America. "All South America, and Mexico, and the islands included." I told him I thought Great Britain was not yet prepared for such a direct proposition: and, entering into details, I immediately found it was a crude idea, which he immediately abandoned. But I conjectured that either [Caesar] Rodney and [Henry M.] Brackenridge [would be interested].

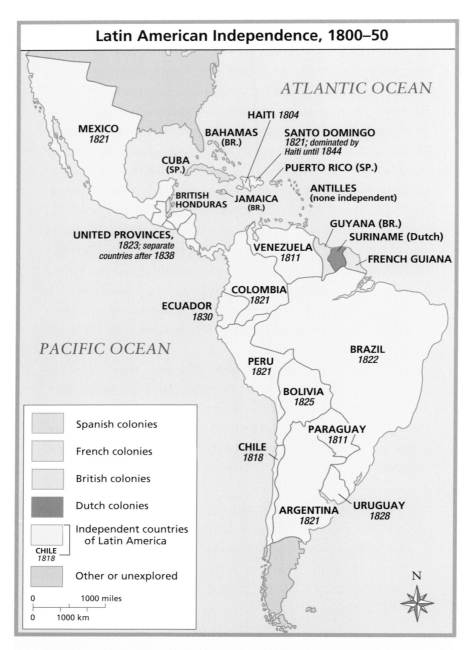

Latin American Independence, 1800–50

ATLANTIC OCEAN

HAITI *1804*

MEXICO
1821

BAHAMAS
(BR.)

SANTO DOMINGO
*1821; dominated by
Haiti until 1844*

CUBA
(SP.)

PUERTO RICO (SP.)

BRITISH
HONDURAS

JAMAICA
(BR.)

ANTILLES
(none independent)

UNITED PROVINCES,
*1823; separate
countries after 1838*

VENEZUELA
1811

GUYANA (BR.)
SURINAME (Dutch)

FRENCH GUIANA

COLOMBIA
1821

ECUADOR
1830

PACIFIC OCEAN

BRAZIL
1822

PERU
1821

BOLIVIA
1825

PARAGUAY
1811

CHILE
1818

ARGENTINA
1821

URUGUAY
1828

Spanish colonies

French colonies

British colonies

Dutch colonies

Independent countries
of Latin America

CHILE
1818

Other or unexplored

0   1000 miles

0   1000 km

N

As depicted on this map of Latin America, the majority of South American countries achieved independence in the 1820s. It was during this period that the
Monroe Doctrine became the cornerstone of U.S. foreign policy.

Caesar Rodney (nephew of the signer of the Declaration of Independence who bore the same name) was appointed by President Monroe to lead a commission to investigate whether the newly formed South American republics should be recognized. He strongly advocated such recognition and, with John Graham, published his findings in 1819 as *Reports on the Present State of the United Provinces of South America.* Rodney was eventually, in 1823, appointed U.S. envoy to the United Provinces of La Plata, now known as Argentina. Henry M. Brackenridge was an attorney and judge who carried out early diplomatic missions for Monroe in South America. Both these men were early and staunch advocates for the United States doing all it could to assure the security of the new Latin American republics. Monroe was to receive similar encouragement and support from such newspapers as the *Richmond Enquirer*, lobbying for American action, or at least American rhetoric, in defense of liberty in the South American hemisphere.

It must be said that, at first, John Quincy Adams was lukewarm on the idea that eventually coalesced into the Monroe Doctrine. "We have our own house to tend to," he wrote one of his sons, "our own coast to shore up. We should, I think, be wary and tread lightly." Adams would, however, come around soon enough.

The Doctrine
Emerges

During mid-1823, British foreign secretary George Canning made a startling proposal to President James Monroe and Secretary of State John Quincy Adams, via the American minister to Great Britain, Richard Rush. "Is not the moment come when our Governments might understand each other as to the Spanish American Colonies? And if we can arrive at such an understanding, would it not be expedient for ourselves, and beneficial for all the world, that the principles of it should be clearly settled and plainly avowed?"

Canning stated flatly that the Crown conceived the recovery of the colonies by Spain to be hopeless and pointless, and that it was only a matter of time before the countries of the world recognized the new republics as independent states. "We are, however, by no means disposed to throw any impediment in the way of an arrangement between them, and the mother country, by

In 1823, British foreign secretary George Canning (depicted here) proposed that the United States and Great Britain should jointly protect the
newly independent South American countries. However, the United States
was more interested in unilateral protection of these countries.

amicable negotiation. . . . We aim not at the possession of any portion of them ourselves . . . [and] we could not see any portion of them transferred to any other Power, with indifference," Canning stated.

"If these opinions and feelings are as I firmly believe them to be, common to your Government with ours," Canning continued, "why should we hesitate mutually to confide them to each other; and to declare them in the face of the world? If there be any European Power which cherishes other projects, which looks to a forcible enterprise for reducing the Colonies to subjugation, on the behalf or in the name of Spain; or which meditates the acquisition of any part of them to itself, by cession or by conquest; such a declaration on the part of your government and ours would be at once the most effectual and the least offensive mode of intimating our joint disapprobation of such projects."

Canning added that such an announcement would at the same time "put an end to all the jealousies of Spain with respect to her remaining Colonies—and to the agitation which prevails in those Colonies, an agitation which it would be but humane to allay; being determined (as we are) not to profit by encouraging it. . . . Nothing could be more gratifying to me than to join with you in such a work, and, I am persuaded, there has seldom, in the history of the world, occurred an opportunity when so small an effort, of two friendly Governments, might produce so unequivocal a good and prevent such extensive calamities."

After receiving this message in October, Monroe went to his home in Virginia. During this brief hiatus, he consulted Thomas Jefferson at Monticello and James Madison at his home, Montpelier. Jefferson advised Monroe to accept the British proposal. Madison was more tepid and leaned toward Secretary Adams's view that Great Britain's suggestion was inspired more by her own self-interest than by any general principle of liberty.

INITIAL DEBATE

Canning's proposal took up the entire meeting of Monroe's cabinet on November 7. "Cabinet meeting at the President's from half past one till four," Adams wrote in his diary. He continued:

On November 7, 1823, James Monroe's (center) cabinet met to discuss George Canning's plan of joint protection over South America. Ultimately, the cabinet (from left to right: Secretary of State John Quincy Adams, Secretary of the Treasury William H. Crawford, Attorney General William Wirt, Secretary of War John Caldwell Calhoun, Secretary of the Navy Samuel Southard, and Postmaster General John McLean) rejected the British offer.

Mr. Calhoun, Secretary of War, and Mr. Southard, Secretary of the Navy, present. The subject for consideration was, the confidential proposals of the British Secretary of State, George Canning, to R. Rush, and the correspondence between them relating to the projects of the Holy Alliance [Russia, Prussia, and Austria] upon South America. There was much conversation, without coming to any definite point. The object of Canning appears to have been to obtain some public pledge from the Government of the United States, ostensibly against the forcible interference of the Holy Alliance between Spain and South America; but really or especially against the acquisition to the United States themselves of any part of the Spanish American possessions.

THE HOLY ALLIANCE

During 1815, an alliance was created between Great Britain, Russia, Austria, and Prussia (Germany) to combat Napoleon's army in Europe. After Napoleon's ultimate defeat at the Battle of Waterloo in June of that year, Tsar Alexander of Russia was largely responsible for establishing the world's first modern peacekeeping organization by uniting the European monarchies into a coalition. The so-called "Holy Alliance" included virtually every monarchy in Europe, with the exception of Great Britain, which Alexander criticized as being a constitutional monarchy rather than a supreme autocracy. (Thus, Great Britain was, in Alexander's view, corrupted by the emerging influence of popular government, which Alexander believed was virtually the same as socialism.) Officially, the Holy Alliance was established to promote peace through the spread of the teachings of Jesus Christ.

However, the Holy Alliance was more than that; it existed to maintain, enhance, and spread the powers of traditional autocratic monarchies. To Tsar Alexander and other leaders of the alliance, democracy equaled anarchy, bloodshed, revolution, and heresy. Popular government, in the view of the leaders of the Holy Alliance, meant the seizing of power by the rabble from God-anointed sovereigns, in defiance of the "Divine Right" of kings. With their combined armies and fleets, the Holy Alliance worked successfully to defeat would-be republican governments in the states of Italy. The might of the Holy Alliance also helped restore Ferdinand VII to power in Spain after the constitutional movement of 1812 had threatened to end his rule. On June 2, 1823, James Madison wrote to Thomas Jefferson about France's move to quell the revolution in Spain:

> The French armies have entered Spain and thus the Bourbon family has put at issue by an offensive movement its own fortune, perhaps its existence for should the attack fail, they will

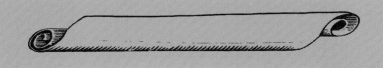

have no claim on the justice, if on the liberality of any portion of these, even in France at whose vital interests the blow was aimed. What the precise organization of the revolutionary force in Spain is, or whether any is formed in France, are facts with which we have little knowledge. We cannot believe that the revolutionary spirit has become extinct in the latter country, after the astonishing feats performed in favor of liberty by Frenchmen in latter days, nor can we suppose that the governing power in Spain would have risked so much, or could have gone so far, had it not relied on the support of the nation. . . . Should the French armies be repulsed, and a party in France declare, in favor of going Bonaparte, it is probable that Austria would at least be paralyzed, if she did not take part with him. That any thing of a bolder stamp would be now practicable, there is much cause to doubt. Such is the state of Europe, & our relation to it is pretty much the same, as it was in the commencement of the French revolution. Can we, in any form take a bolder attitude in regard to it, in favor of liberty, than we then did? Can we afford greater aid to that cause by assuming any such attitude, than we now do, by the force of our example? These are subjects, on which I should be glad to hear your sentiments.

Calhoun was inclined to giving a discretionary power to Rush to join in a declaration against the interference of the Holy Alliance, if necessary, even if it should pledge the United States not to take Cuba or the province of Texas "because the power of Great Britain being greater than ours to *seize* upon them, we should get the advantage of obtaining from her the same declaration we should make ourselves."

However, Adams thought the cases not to be parallel. "We have no intention of seizing either Texas or Cuba," he noted. "But the inhabitants of either or both may exercise their primitive fights, and solicit a union with us. They will certainly do no such thing to Great Britain. By joining with her, therefore, in her proposed declaration, we give her a substantial and perhaps inconvenient pledge against ourselves, and really obtain nothing in return. Without entering now into the enquiry of the expediency of our annexing Texas or Cuba to our Union, we should at least keep ourselves free to act as emergencies may arise, and not tie ourselves down to any principle which might immediately afterwards be brought to bear against ourselves."

Southard agreed with Adams, while President Monroe stated his aversion to any course which would give the impression of the United States taking a subordinate position to Great Britain. Adams recalled,

> I remarked that the communications recently received from the Russian Minister, Baron Tuyl, afforded, as I thought, a very suitable and convenient opportunity for us to take our stand against the Holy Alliance, and at the same time to decline the overture of Great Britain. It would be more candid, as well as more dignified, to avow our principles explicitly to Russia and France, than to come in as a cockboat in the wake of the British man-of-war. This idea was acquiesced in on all sides, and my draft for an answer to Baron Tuyl's note announcing the Emperor's determination to refuse receiving any Minister from the South American Governments was read.

A CLAP OF THUNDER

A week later, on November 13, Adams had more interaction with the president on this topic. "I find him [the president] yet altogether unsettled in his own mind as to the answer to be given to Mr. Canning's proposals, and alarmed, far beyond anything that I could have conceived possible, with the fear that the Holy Alliance are about to restore immediately all South America to Spain. . . . He will recover from this in a few days; but I never saw more indecision in him."

Two days later, at a cabinet meeting, Adams noted that Calhoun seemed absolutely "moonstruck" and certain that the Holy Allies, "with ten thousand men," would soon "restore all Mexico and all South America to the Spanish dominion." Adams made it plain that he was not similarly impressed:

> I didn't deny that they might make a temporary impression for three, four, or five years, but I no more believe that the Holy Allies will restore Spanish dominion upon the American continent than that the Chimborazo [Ecuador's highest peak] will sink beneath the ocean. But, I added, if the South Americans were really in a state to be so easily subdued, it would be but a more forcible motive for us to beware of involving ourselves in their fate. I set this down as one of Calhoun's extravagances. He is for plunging into a war to prevent that which, if his opinion of it is correct, we are utterly unable to prevent. He is for earmarking our lives and fortunes in a ship which he declares the very rats have abandoned.

During a later cabinet meeting held on November 21, Monroe offered a draft of a proposed message that included praise of the Greek rebels in their revolt against Turkey and also a lecture for the French, scolding them for their invasion of Spain. Adams opposed specific references to Greece and Spain. Rather, the United States should take an independent stand, emphasizing the idea of two hemispheres and America's complete separation from Europe. Monroe agreed to rewrite his message to be delivered to Congress for maximum publicity. As Adams recalled:

> The President . . . taking up the sketches that he had prepared for his message, read them to us. Its introduction was in a tone of deep solemnity and of high alarm, intimating that

the country is menaced by imminent and formidable dangers, such as would probably soon call for the most vigorous energies and the closest union. It then proceeded to speak of the foreign affairs, chiefly according to the sketch I had given him some days since, but with occasional variations. It then alluded to the recent events in Spain and Portugal, speaking in terms of the most pointed reprobation of the late invasion of Spain by France, and of the principles upon which it was undertaken by the open avowal of the King of France. It also contained a broad acknowledgement to the Greeks as an independent nation, and a recommendation to Congress to make an appropriation for sending a Minister to them. Of all this Mr. Calhoun declared his approbation. I expressed as freely my wish that the President would reconsider the whole subject before he should determine to take that course. I said the tone of the introduction I apprehended would take the nation by surprise and greatly alarm them. It would come upon them like a clap of thunder. There had never been in the history of this nation a period of so deep calm and tranquility as we now enjoyed. We never were, upon the whole, in a state of peace so profound and secure with all foreign nations as at this time. This message would be a summons to arms—to arms against all of Europe, and for objects of policy exclusively European—Greece and Spain. It would be as new, too, in our policy as it would be surprising.

THE FINAL LANGUAGE EVOLVES

During a gathering of the cabinet on November 26, Adams made the point that if the Holy Alliance really did invade "South America, especially Mexico, it was impossible, in the nature of things, that they should do it to restore the old exclusive dominion of Spain." He continued,

Spain had not, and never could again have, the physical force to maintain that dominion; and if the countries should be kept in subjugation by the armies of the Allies, was it in human absurdity to imagine that they should waste their blood and treasure to prohibit their own subjects upon pain of death to set foot upon those territories? Surely not. If then the Holy Allies should subdue Spanish America, however they might at first set up the standard of Spain, the ultimate result of their undertaking would be to recolonize them, partitioned out among themselves. . . . And Great Britain, as her last resort, if she could not resist this course of things, would take at least the island of Cuba for her share of the scramble.

Adams went on to postulate yet another scenario. "Suppose the Holy Allies should attack South America," he said, "and Great Britain should resist them alone and without our cooperation. I thought this not an improbable contingency, and I believed in such a struggle the allies would be defeated and Great Britain would be victorious, by her command of the sea. But, as the independence of the South Americans would then be only protected by the guarantee of Great Britain, it would throw them completely into her arms, and in the result make them her colonies instead of those of Spain." Adams believed that the United States must act "promptly and decisively" to articulate a policy that would put South American intervention off-bounds for *all* non-American powers, whether France, Spain, Russia, or Great Britain. This, in the end, was to be Adams's great contribution to the proceedings. Here was the flash of genius, the core idea of what would become the Monroe Doctrine: Europe should keep its hands off the American continent.

THE DOCTRINE PRONOUNCED

On the day James Monroe sent his message to Congress— December 2, 1823—John Quincy Adams paid several calls around Washington on other business. During a confidential

HENRY   CLAY.

Speaker of the House of Representatives Henry Clay, who is depicted in this Currier and Ives lithograph, supported the Monroe Doctrine as it related to U.S. foreign policy. The founder of the Whig Party was a "war hawk" and favored U.S. intervention in foreign affairs.

chat, Henry Clay told Adams the part of the president's message related to foreign affairs "was, he thought, the best part . . . He thought the Government had weakened itself and the tone of the country by withholding so long the acknowledgment of the South American independence, and he believed even a war for it against all Europe, including even England, would be advantageous to us." Adams was not so sure. "I told him I believed a war for South American independence might be inevitable, and, under certain circumstances, might be expedient, but that I viewed war in a very different light from him—as necessarily placing high interests of different portions of the Union at odds with each other, and thereby endangering the Union itself."

Two days later, Adams called at the Executive Mansion and found the editor of the *National Intelligencer* there. "He said the [president's message to Congress] was called a war message; and spoke of newspaper paragraphs from Europe announcing that an army of twelve thousand Spaniards was to embark immediately to subdue South America." Adams was having none of this. "I told him there was absurdity on the face of these paragraphs, as the same newspapers announced with more authenticity the disbanding of the Spanish army. The President himself is singularly disturbed with these rumors of invasion by the Holy Alliance."

Interestingly, however, it would be more than 20 years before another president—James K. Polk, speaking in 1845—actually coined the phrase "Monroe Doctrine." James Monroe himself never knew the phrase, although John Quincy Adams lived long enough to hear the name applied to the policy he had wrought so many years before. "I believe," the elderly Adams wrote, "that it will wear well through the years, and deliver good service not only to the United States, but to mankind. In crafting something of use in our own time, our immediate moment, we may well have designed a device that will last and be of service through the centuries. I hope so."

The Doctrine
Grows Up

As John Quincy Adams foresaw, the Monroe Doctrine took on a life of its own during subsequent administrations. Its two core ideas held true through the years. First, that the United States would not tolerate European powers further colonizing the American continents and that they should not interfere with the newly independent Spanish American republics. And second, that the United States would not interfere in existing European colonies or in Europe itself. Implicit was Adams's newly shaped concept of an American sphere of influence.

Without the existence of the Monroe Doctrine, the history of Latin America, not to mention the history of the world, would have been completely different, just as the map of contemporary South America would be completely different as well. Without the Monroe Doctrine, Latin America would likely have been sliced into portions to serve the colonial needs of a range of European powers, not just Spain. Other European countries—among them Holland, Germany, France, and Great Britain—would have gained a major foothold, introducing not only new lines to the map, but also new languages and cultures. In sum, what the Monroe Doctrine accomplished in large measure was to allow the seed of Spanish culture to develop in South America without many other foreign influences.

THE POLK DOCTRINE

As has been noted previously, the first president to give a name to Monroe's and Adams's invention—the Monroe Doctrine—was James K. Polk. During 1845, Polk successfully invoked the doctrine against British threats in California and Oregon, as well as against French and British efforts to prevent the United States' annexation of Texas. (A large part of the British calculus in acquiescing on the West Coast and in Texas was the fact that they happily supported the Monroe Doctrine when applied to Latin America, where the British were opposed to colonization by European powers.)

In his message to Congress on December 2, 1845, President Polk expanded the Monroe Doctrine to incorporate American ambitions involving manifest destiny. This version of the Monroe Doctrine came to be known as the Polk Doctrine. Where Monroe had indicated that the Western Hemisphere was not available for European colonialism, Polk expanded on this to make clear that the United States would not allow Europeans to interfere with U.S. territorial ambitions in the same hemisphere. "It is submitted to the wisdom of Congress," said Polk,

> to determine whether, at their present session, and until after the expiration of the year's notice, any other measures may be adopted consistently with the convention of 1827 for the security of our rights and the government and protection of our citizens in Oregon. That it will ultimately be wise and

In his address to Congress on December 2, 1845, President James K. Polk used the Monroe Doctrine to champion his policy of manifest destiny. Polk believed the United States should annex the territories of Texas and Oregon, as well as take Mexico.

proper to make liberal grants of land to the patriotic pioneers, who amidst privations and dangers lead the way through savage tribes inhabiting the vast wilderness intervening between our frontier settlements and Oregon, and who cultivate and are ever ready to defend the soil, I am fully satisfied. To doubt whether they will obtain such grants as soon as the convention between the United States and Great Britain shall have ceased to exist would be to doubt the justice of Congress; but, pending the year's notice, it is worthy of consideration whether a stipulation to this effect may be made consistently with the spirit of that convention. . . .

At the end of the year's notice, should Congress think it proper to make provision for giving that notice, we shall have reached a period when the national rights in Oregon must either be abandoned or firmly maintained. That they cannot be abandoned without a sacrifice of both national honor and interest is too clear to admit of doubt.

Oregon is a part of the North American continent, to which, it is confidently affirmed, the title of the United States is the best now in existence. For the grounds on which that title rests I refer you to the correspondence of the late and present secretary of state with the British plenipotentiary [envoy] during the negotiation. The British proposition of compromise, which would make the Columbia the line south of 49 degrees, with a trifling addition of detached territory to the United States north of that river, and would leave on the British side two-thirds of the whole Oregon territory, including the free navigation of the Columbia and all the valuable harbors on the Pacific, can never for a moment be entertained by the United States without an abandonment of their just and clear territorial rights, their own self-respect, and the national honor. . . .

The rapid extension of our settlements over our territories heretofore unoccupied, the addition of new states to our confederacy, the expansion of free principles, and our rising greatness as a nation are attracting the attention of the powers of Europe, and lately the doctrine has been broached in some of them of a "balance of power" on this continent to check our advancement. The United States, sincerely desirous of preserving relations of good understanding with all nations, cannot in silence permit any European interference on the North American continent, and should any such interference be attempted will be ready to resist it at any and all hazards.

It is well known to the American people and to all nations that this government has never interfered with the relations subsisting between other governments. We have never made ourselves parties to their wars or their alliances; we have not sought their territories by conquest; we have not mingled with parties in their domestic struggles; and believing our own form of government to be the best, we have never attempted to propagate it by intrigues, by diplomacy, or by force. We may claim on this continent a like exemption from European interference. The nations of America are equally sovereign and independent with those of Europe. They possess the same rights, independent of all foreign interposition, to make war, to conclude peace, and to regulate their internal affairs. The people of the United States cannot, therefore, view with indifference attempts of European powers to interfere with the independent action of the nations on this continent.

The American system of government is entirely different from that of Europe. Jealousy among the different sovereigns of Europe, lest any one of them might become too powerful for the rest, has caused them anxiously to desire the establishment of what they term the "balance of power." It cannot be permitted to have any application on the North American continent, and especially to the United States. We must ever maintain the principle that the people of this continent alone have the right to decide their own destiny. Should any portion of them, constituting an independent state, propose to unite themselves with our confederacy, this will be a question for them and us to determine without any foreign interposition. We can never consent that European powers shall interfere to prevent such a union because it might disturb the "balance of power" which they may desire to maintain upon this continent.

Near a quarter of a century ago the principle was distinctly announced to the world, in the annual message of one of my predecessors, that: The American continents, by the free and independent condition which they have assumed and maintain, are henceforth not to be considered as subjects for future colonization by any European powers.

This principle will apply with greatly increased force should any European power attempt to establish any new colony in North America. In the existing circumstances of the world the present is deemed a proper occasion to reiterate and reaffirm the principle avowed by Mr. Monroe and to state my cordial concurrence in its wisdom and sound policy. The reassertion of this principle, especially in reference to North America, is at this day but the promulgation of a policy which no European power should cherish the disposition to resist. Existing rights of every European nation should be respected, but it is due alike to our safety and our interests that the efficient protection of our laws should be extended over our whole territorial limits, and that it should be distinctly announced to the world as our settled policy that no future European colony or dominion shall with our consent be planted or established on any part of the North American continent.

Three years later, Polk once again invoked the Monroe Doctrine when he warned against European interloping on the Yucatán Peninsula in Mexico. Polk insisted that any imperial effort by any European power in that region would cause the United States to move in and seize the terrain for itself.

Throughout the late nineteenth century, different historical situations led to significantly different levels of commitment to the Monroe Doctrine. Between the years 1861 and 1865, the enormous distraction of the U.S. Civil War greatly reduced the Union government's ability both to monitor events in South America and to convincingly threaten military enforcement of the doctrine. Thus, while Northerners and Southerners fought each other at the battles of Shiloh and Gettysburg, Spain was able to reassert control in the Dominican Republic (1861) just as France was able to intervene in Mexico (1862–67) to support the imperialist leader Maximilian.

THE DOCTRINE MATURES

President Ulysses S. Grant and the chief executives after him gradually revised, refined, and expanded the Monroe Doctrine. The concept eventually grew to include the idea that no territory anywhere in the Western Hemisphere could be transferred from one European power to another. Later on, as the United States' own imperialistic impulses became apparent, the Monroe Doctrine found itself expanded even further. In time, the exclusion of European interlopers in the Western Hemisphere was expanded to become an exclusion of all non-American powers. At the same time, however, the United States voiced its own right to expansion in the hemisphere wherever necessary. Thus, the Monroe Doctrine eventually came to be viewed with suspicion by many Latin American citizens and leaders.

During 1895, President Grover Cleveland revised and extended the Monroe Doctrine yet again when he demanded Great Britain submit to arbitration to resolve a boundary dispute between Venezuela and British Guiana (now Guyana).

THE VENEZUELA CLAIMS CRISIS

In the year 1902, Venezuela was in the midst of a financial crisis caused by civil unrest and unsound monetary policies embarked upon by Venezuelan leader Cipriano Castro. The result was that Venezuela had to default on loans owed to a range of European governments, among them Great Britain, Germany, and Italy. Intent on seeing that Venezuela made good on the loans, the

In 1895, President Grover Cleveland revised and extended the Monroe Doctrine by adopting a policy that went beyond prohibiting European colonization in Latin America. Cleveland believed that the United States should have a say in all matters related to Latin American countries when it came to European intervention.

three powers dispatched a combined naval expedition to blockade and bombard Venezuelan seaports and capture Venezuelan merchant ships along with gunboats of the Venezuelan Navy.

This action represented a gross and bold violation of the Monroe Doctrine, even though the European powers loudly announced that they harbored no territorial ambitions in Venezuela or anywhere else in South America and that they merely intended to collect on money owed. Early in the process, President Theodore Roosevelt declined a request that the United States take on the role of arbitrator between Venezuela and the European bill collectors. Nevertheless, through back channels, the United States did seek to facilitate a settlement that all parties would agree to.

The claims against Venezuela were adjusted during a conference held at Caracas in 1903. However, further debate then arose as to whether Venezuela should make it a priority to pay off the three blockading powers or to pay the blockading parties at the same rate they paid other nations. During 1904, the International Court of Arbitration at the Hague decided in favor of Venezuela paying the blockading nations first. The dispute became unique in the history of international law, because the Monroe Doctrine had never previously been extended to such a case. It also made history because the great resentment of Spanish American nations over the shared violation of the sovereignty resulted in the Drago Doctrine, considered to be the South American corollary to the Monroe Doctrine.

Articulated in 1902 by the renowned Argentinean diplomat Luis María Drago in protest to the blockade by Great Britain, Germany, and Italy, the Drago Doctrine held that no debt should ever be collected from a South American state by a foreign power through the use of armed force or through the occupation of territory. The Drago Doctrine was eventually brought up and debated at the Pan-American Congress of 1906. One year later, it was brought up again before the International Hague Conference of 1907, where a modified form offered by American diplomat Horace Porter eventually won approval.

LET IT BE WRITTEN SO IT CAN BE READ.—From the *Herald* (New York).

Entitled "Let It Be Written So It Can Be Read," this political cartoon appeared in the *New York Herald* in 1904. The cartoon depicts European rulers observing U.S. naval might in protecting its interests through the application of the Monroe Doctrine.

How the matter of the Venezuela claims came to arbitration is an interesting one that reveals much about the wit and character of Theodore Roosevelt. The writer William Roscoe Thayer, who was a friend of Roosevelt's, tells the tale:

> The people of Venezuela owed considerable sums to merchants and bankers in Germany, England, and Italy, and the creditors could recover neither their capital nor the interest on it. The Kaiser bethought himself of the simple plan of making a naval demonstration against the Venezuelans if

they did not pay up; he would send his troops ashore, occupy the chief harbors, and take in the customs. To disguise his ulterior motive, he persuaded England and Italy to join him in collecting their bill against Venezuela. So warships of the three nations appeared off the Venezuelan coast, and for some time they maintained what they called "A peaceful blockade." After a while Secretary [of State] [John] Hay pointed out that there could be no such thing as a peaceful blockade; that a blockade was, by its very nature, an act of war; accordingly the blockaders declared a state of belligerency between themselves and Venezuela, and Germany threatened to bombard the seacoast towns unless the debt was settled without further delay. President Roosevelt had no illusions as to what bombardment and occupation by German troops would mean. If a regiment or two of Germans once went into garrison at Caracas or Porto Cabello, the Kaiser would secure the foothold he craved on the American Coast within striking distance of the projected Canal, and Venezuela, unable to ward off his aggression, would certainly be helpless to drive him out. Mr. Roosevelt allowed Mr. Herbert W. Bowen, the American Minister to Venezuela, to serve as Special Commissioner for Venezuela in conducting her negotiations with Germany. He, himself, however, took the matter into his own hands at Washington. Having sounded England and Italy, and learned that they were willing to arbitrate, and knowing also that neither of them schemed to take territorial payment for their bills, he directed his diplomatic attack straight at the Kaiser. When the German Ambassador, Dr. von Holleben, one of the pompous and ponderous professorial sort of German officials, was calling on him at the White House, the President told him to warn the Kaiser that unless he consented, within a given time—about ten days—to arbitrate the Venezuelan dispute, the American fleet under Admiral Dewey would appear off the Venezuelan coast and defend it from any attack which the German Squadron might attempt to make. Holleben displayed consternation; he protested that since his Imperial Master had refused to arbitrate, there could be no arbitration. His Imperial Master could not change his Imperial Mind, and the dutiful servant asked the President whether he realized what such a demand meant. The President replied calmly that he knew it meant war. A week passed, but brought no reply from Berlin; then Holleben called again at the White House on some unimportant matters; as he turned to go the President inquired, "Have you heard from Berlin?" "No," said Holleben. "Of course His Imperial Majesty cannot arbitrate." "Very well," said Roosevelt, "you may think it worth while to cable to Berlin that I have changed my mind. I am sending instructions to Admiral Dewey to take our fleet to Venezuela next Monday instead of Tuesday." Holleben brought the interview to a close at once and departed with evident signs of alarm. He returned in less than thirty-six hours with relief and satisfaction written on his face, as he informed the President, "His Imperial Majesty consents to arbitrate."

The Roosevelt Corollary and the Twentieth Century

In his annual message to Congress, December 6, 1904, Theodore Roosevelt enunciated what has come to be known as the Roosevelt Corollary to the Monroe Doctrine. In the aftermath of the Venezuela claims crisis, Roosevelt stated that unrest of any kind in a Latin American country, or international misbehavior that invited the intervention of European powers, might in turn force the United States to intervene preemptively in this region in order to prevent European powers from doing the same. This interpretation—with all of its frankly imperialistic overtones—gained favor with a range of subsequent U.S. presidents, who deployed the Roosevelt Corollary to justify interventions—both overt and covert—in the Caribbean and throughout South America.

AN ADDITION TO THE MONROE DOCTRINE

"It is not true," Roosevelt stated in his message, "that the United States feels any land hunger or entertains any projects as regards the other nations of the Western Hemisphere save such as are for their welfare." He continued:

> All that this country desires is to see the neighboring countries stable, orderly, and prosperous. Any country whose people conduct themselves well can count upon our hearty friendship. If a nation shows that it knows how to act with reasonable efficiency and decency in social and political matters, if it keeps order and pays its obligations, it need fear no interference from the United States. Chronic wrongdoing, or an impotence which results in a general loosening of the ties of civilized society, may in America, as elsewhere, ultimately require intervention by some civilized nation, and in the Western Hemisphere the adherence of the United States to the Monroe Doctrine may force the United States, however reluctantly, in flagrant cases of such wrongdoing or impotence, to the exercise of an international police power. If every country washed by the Caribbean Sea would show the progress in stable and just civilization which with the aid of the Platt amendment Cuba has shown since our troops left the island, and which so many of the republics in both Americas are constantly and brilliantly showing, all question of interference by this Nation with their affairs would be at an end. Our interests and those of our southern neighbors are in reality identical. They have great natural riches, and if within their borders the reign of law and justice obtains, prosperity is sure to come to them. While they thus obey the primary laws of civilized society they may rest assured that they will be treated by us in a spirit of cordial and helpful sympathy. We would interfere with them only in the last resort and then only if it became evident that their inability or unwillingness to do

justice at home and abroad had violated the rights of the United States or had invited foreign aggression to the detriment of the entire body of American nations. It is a mere truism to say that every nation, whether in America or anywhere else, which desires to maintain its freedom, its independence, must ultimately realize that the right of such independence can not be separated from the responsibility of making good use of it. In asserting the Monroe Doctrine, in taking such steps as we have taken in regard to Cuba, Venezuela, and Panama, and in endeavoring to circumscribe the theater of war in the Far East, and to secure the open door in China, we have acted in our own interest as well as in the interest of humanity at large. There are, however, cases in which, while our own interests are not greatly involved, strong appeal is made to our sympathies. . . . But in extreme cases action may be justifiable and proper. What form the action shall take must depend upon the circumstances of the case; that is, upon the degree of the atrocity and upon our power to remedy it. The cases in which we could interfere by force of arms as we interfered to put a stop to intolerable conditions in Cuba [at the time of the Spanish American War in 1898] are necessarily very few.

In his address, Roosevelt insisted that the United States would intervene whenever necessary to guarantee that other nations in the Western Hemisphere fulfilled their obligations to international creditors. In this way, the United States would make sure to guarantee its sphere of influence, and deflect the possibility of invasions by foreign interlopers. As the corollary took shape in reality, however, it added up to steadily increased U.S. military police action throughout the Caribbean and South America, as Roosevelt and his heirs in office worked to create stability within the fractured and random governments of the area. In his message to Congress, Roosevelt had insisted that the United States would "exercise international police power in 'flagrant cases of such wrongdoing or impotence.'" But in truth,

In 1904, President Theodore Roosevelt added the Roosevelt Corollary to the Monroe Doctrine. Roosevelt's addition stated that the United States had the right to intervene in the affairs of a Latin American nation when said nation committed some kind of wrongdoing.

over the long decades, the Roosevelt Corollary had much less to do with insulating the Western Hemisphere from European intervention than it did with justifying the United States' own intervening in the internal affairs of such governments as Cuba, Nicaragua, Haiti, and the Dominican Republic.

THE UNITED STATES IN LATIN AMERICA

So that Latin American states might respect their "international obligations and justice towards foreigners" and to "bring about progress and democracy for backward people," U.S. soldiers eventually landed—at various points in time—in places ranging from Mexico, Guatemala, and Nicaragua, to Colombia and Ecuador. As Theodore Roosevelt's successor, William Howard Taft, said in 1912: "The whole hemisphere

(continues on page 108)

THEODORE ROOSEVELT COMMENTS ON THE MONROE DOCTRINE

In 1904, President Theodore Roosevelt established a corollary, or addition, to the Monroe Doctrine that stated that the United States could intervene in the internal affairs of any Latin American country if that country was responsible for any wrongdoing. In essence, the United States began policing the Americas so that European nations would not interfere in the affairs of Latin American countries. The following excerpt that defines Roosevelt's view on the Monroe Doctrine is from his autobiography, which was published in 1913 by Macmillan:

> The Monroe Doctrine lays down the rule that the Western Hemisphere is not hereafter to be treated as subject to settlement and occupation by Old World powers. It is not international law; but it is a cardinal principle of our foreign policy. There is no difficulty at the present day in maintaining this doctrine, save where the American power whose interest is threatened has shown itself in international matters both weak and delinquent. The great and prosperous civilized commonwealths, such as the Argentine, Brazil, and Chile, in the Southern half of South America, have advanced so far that they no longer stand in any position of tutelage toward the United States. They occupy toward us precisely the position that Canada occupies. Their friendship is the friendship of equals for equals. My view was that as regards these nations there was no more necessity for asserting the Monroe Doctrine than there was to assert it in regard to Canada. They were competent to assert it for themselves. Of course if one of these nations, or if Canada, should be overcome by some Old World power, which then proceeded to occupy its territory, we would undoubtedly, if the American Nation needed our help, give it in order to prevent such occupation from taking place. But the initiative would come from the

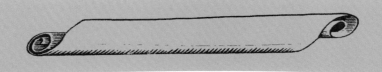

Nation itself, and the United States would merely act as a friend whose help was invoked.

The case was (and is) widely different as regards certain—not all—of the tropical states in the neighborhood of the Caribbean Sea. Where these states are stable and prosperous, they stand on a footing of absolute equality with all other communities. But some of them have been a prey to such continuous revolutionary misrule as to have grown impotent either to do their duties to outsiders or to enforce their rights against outsiders. The United States has not the slightest desire to make aggressions on any one of these states. On the contrary, it will submit to much from them without showing resentment. If any great civilized power, Russia or Germany, for instance, had behaved toward us as Venezuela under Castro behaved, this country would have gone to war at once. We did not go to war with Venezuela merely because our people declined to be irritated by the actions of a weak opponent, and showed a forbearance which probably went beyond the limits of wisdom in refusing to take umbrage at what was done by the weak; although we would certainly have resented it had it been done by the strong. . . .

. . . but whenever a sufficiently strong outside nation becomes sufficiently aggrieved, then either that nation will act or the United States Government itself will have to act. We were face to face at one period of my administration with this condition of affairs in Venezuela, when Germany, rather feebly backed by England, undertook a blockade against Venezuela to make Venezuela adopt the German and English view about certain agreements. There was real danger that the blockade would finally result in Germany's taking possession of certain cities or custom-houses. I succeeded, however, in getting all the parties in interest to submit their cases to the Hague Tribunal.

(continued from page 105)

will be ours in fact as, by virtue of our superiority of race, it already is ours morally."

Under this umbrella of U.S. protectionism, the American-owned United Fruit Company made a massive investment and created a highly profitable banana empire in eastern and northern Colombia, Central America, and Venezuela. The millions of acres owned by the United Fruit Company represented incredibly lucrative sovereign, independent, corporate states within states. To protect the United Fruit monopoly, the government of the United States routinely used its full intelligence apparatus, diplomatic talents, and military power—backed by the logic of the Roosevelt Corollary—to co-opt the internal affairs of South America and turn their domestic politics in directions favorable to United Fruit and its investors.

The governments in question were troubled, tangled affairs. Never far from the grip of anarchy and the crimes of political and financial corruption, they were in turn easy to control and manipulate for the benefit of American interests. During Roosevelt's own presidency, the chief focus of American "diplomacy" in South America was to facilitate the building of—and assure American control of—a great canal through Panama linking the Atlantic and Pacific oceans. When the government of Colombia proved unwilling to facilitate American dominion over the project, American agents assisted in the formation of a new, independent state (Panama) that was willing to do business with the United States.

In exchange for $10 million, the government of Panama—via the Hay-Bunau-Varilla Treaty of November 18, 1903—surrendered the canal to the control of the United States in perpetuity, along with a five-mile zone on either shore. In 1926, a further Treaty of Alliance expanded and consolidated American control of the canal zone. Article VI of that treaty granted the United States special rights to enforce security and restrict traffic in time of war and—for all practical purposes—made Panama

Under President Franklin D. Roosevelt, the Monroe Doctrine was once again redefined. However, FDR had more liberal intentions: he supported a Good Neighbor Policy with Latin American countries and emphasized Pan-Americanism, or cooperation, among American nations.

a state of the Union, albeit one without guaranteed rights, and without the right to vote.

A succession of U.S. interventions followed through the coming decades.

THE MONROE DOCTRINE CHANGES SHAPE

Under President Franklin Delano Roosevelt, the Monroe Doctrine was redefined and liberalized, at least somewhat. FDR enunciated a more moderate stance toward relations with South America, termed the *Good Neighbor Policy,* and placed

(continues on page 112)

FRANKLIN ROOSEVELT'S "ARSENAL OF DEMOCRACY" SPEECH

One of President Franklin D. Roosevelt's most famous fireside chats was his "Arsenal of Democracy" speech given on December 29, 1940. In the speech, Roosevelt called for the American people to support European and Asian citizens, who were being subjected to rule by the Fascist regimes of Japan, Germany, and Italy. Perhaps more importantly, Roosevelt emphasized the fact that it was time for the United States to move away from isolationism and build up its infrastructure in preparation for war:

> One hundred and seventeen years ago the Monroe Doctrine was conceived by our Government as a measure of defense in the face of a threat against this hemisphere by an alliance in Continental Europe. Thereafter, we stood [on] guard in the Atlantic, with the British as neighbors. There was no treaty. There was no "unwritten agreement."
>
> And yet, there was the feeling, proven correct by history, that we as neighbors could settle any disputes in peaceful fashion. And the fact is that during the whole of this time the Western Hemisphere has remained free from aggression from Europe or from Asia.
>
> Does anyone seriously believe that we need to fear attack anywhere in the Americas while a free Britain remains our most powerful naval neighbor in the Atlantic? And does anyone seriously believe, on the other hand, that we could rest easy if the Axis powers were our neighbors there?
>
> If Great Britain goes down, the Axis powers will control the continents of Europe, Asia, Africa, Australia, and the high seas— and they will be in a position to bring enormous military and naval resources against this hemisphere. It is no exaggeration to

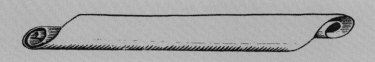

say that all of us, in all the Americas, would be living at the point of a gun—a gun loaded with explosive bullets, economic as well as military.

We should enter upon a new and terrible era in which the whole world, our hemisphere included, would be run by threats of brute force. And to survive in such a world, we would have to convert ourselves permanently into a militaristic power on the basis of war economy.

Some of us like to believe that even if Britain falls, we are still safe, because of the broad expanse of the Atlantic and of the Pacific.

But the width of those [these] oceans is not what it was in the days of clipper ships. At one point between Africa and Brazil the distance is less from Washington than it is from Washington to Denver, Colorado—five hours for the latest type of bomber. And at the North end of the Pacific Ocean America and Asia almost touch each other.

Why, even today we have planes that could fly from the British Isles to New England and back again without refueling. And remember that the range of a modern bomber is ever being increased.

During the past week many people in all parts of the nation have told me what they wanted me to say tonight. Almost all of them expressed a courageous desire to hear the plain truth about the gravity of the situation. One telegram, however . . . begged me not to tell again of the ease with which our American cities could be bombed by any hostile power which had gained bases in this Western Hemisphere.

(continued from page 109)

a focus on hemispheric solidarity against external threats. But after FDR's death in 1945, American adventuring in the internal affairs of states across South America continued and expanded, even though the United States has at the same time supported the work of the Organization of American States (OAS), founded in 1948, to advance common interests and strengthen cooperation among states in South America. At the core of the OAS mission is a devotion to the ideal of democracy. According to the OAS's charter: "The peoples of the Americas have a right to democracy and their governments have an obligation to promote and defend it."

MISSION ACCOMPLISHED

With the economies of South America on a certain footing and those states flourishing as a whole, and with the end of imperial ambitions on the part of both European powers and the United States, the Monroe Doctrine seems an anachronism, a relic of another age. Not only has South America become largely safe within its own borders, but at the same time the United States long ago became the dominant power in the world, with influence and business well beyond its own hemisphere, thus negating one of the two core concepts of Monroe's original vision.

CHRONOLOGY

1758   Birth of James Monroe.

1767   Birth of John Quincy Adams.

1817   James Monroe begins first of two terms as president; John Quincy Adams appointed secretary of state.

1823   Articulation of the Monroe Doctrine to Congress during Monroe's seventh annual State of the Union Address.

1825   John Quincy Adams begins one term as president.

1845   Articulation of the Polk Doctrine (which expanded on the Monroe Doctrine) by President James K. Polk in response to British threats on the West Coast of the United States, and French and British involvement in the possible annexation of Texas.

1848   James K. Polk reasserts the Monroe Doctrine in response to possible European designs on Mexico's Yucatán Peninsula.

1895   President Grover Cleveland uses the Monroe Doctrine to force arbitration of a border dispute between British Guiana and Venezuela.

1901   Theodore Roosevelt begins first term as president.

1902   Venezuelan Claims Crisis and initial articulation of the Drago Doctrine, meant as a corollary to the Monroe Doctrine.

1903–04   Arbitration of the Venezuela claims at the Hague.

1904 Articulation of the Roosevelt Corollary to the Monroe Doctrine by Theodore Roosevelt during his annual meeting with Congress.

1919 President Woodrow Wilson asks for, and receives, an exemption from the terms of the League of Nations for the principle of the Monroe Doctrine.

1928 U.S. State Department promulgates the "Clark Memorandum," which in essence repudiates the Roosevelt Corollary of 1904; memo is published in 1930.

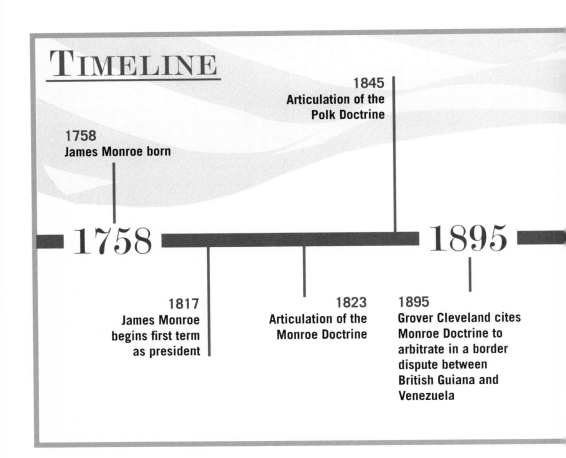

TIMELINE

1845
Articulation of the
Polk Doctrine

1758
James Monroe born

1758   **1895**

1817
James Monroe
begins first term
as president

1823
Articulation of the
Monroe Doctrine

1895
Grover Cleveland cites
Monroe Doctrine to
arbitrate in a border
dispute between
British Guiana and
Venezuela

1933   Franklin D. Roosevelt begins the first term of his presidency and articulates the Good Neighbor Policy during his inaugural address on March 4.

1948   The Organization of American States (OAS) is founded.

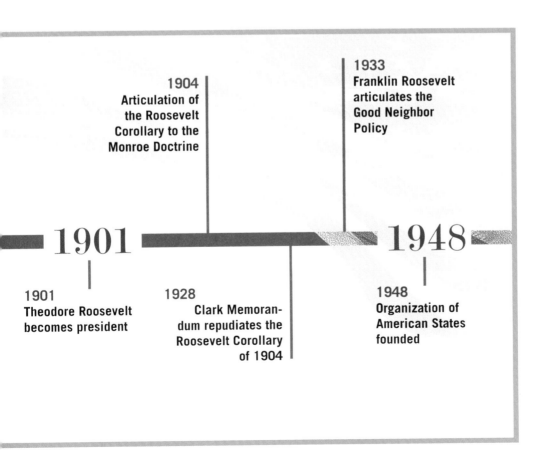

1904
Articulation of
the Roosevelt
Corollary to the
Monroe Doctrine

1933
Franklin Roosevelt
articulates the
Good Neighbor
Policy

1901

1948

1901
Theodore Roosevelt
becomes president

1928
Clark Memoran-
dum repudiates the
Roosevelt Corollary
of 1904

1948
Organization of
American States
founded

BIBLIOGRAPHY

Ammon, Henry. *James Monroe and the Quest for National Identity*. Charlottesville: University of Virginia Press, 1990.

Dangerfield, George. *Defiance of the Old World: The Story Behind the Monroe Doctrine*. New York: Viking Press, 1963.

Donovan, Frank. *Mr. Monroe's Message: The Story Behind the Monroe Doctrine*. New York: Dodd, Mead & Co., 1963.

Merk, Fred. *The Monroe Doctrine and American Expansionism, 1843–1849*. New York: Random House, 1972.

Nagel, Paul C. *John Quincy Adams: A Public Life, A Private Life*. New York: Knopf, 1997.

Perkins, Dexter. *Hands Off: A History of the Monroe Doctrine*. Boston: Little, Brown, 1946.

Smith, Gaddis. *The Last Years of the Monroe Doctrine*. New York: Hill & Wang, 1995.

FURTHER READING

Cunningham, Noble E. *The Presidency of James Monroe.* Lawrence: University Press of Kansas, 1996.

Foster, John W. *A Century of American Diplomacy: A Brief Review of Foreign Relations of the United States, 1776 to 1886.* New York: Kessinger Publishing, 2004.

Hart, Gary. *James Monroe (American Presidents Series).* New York: Times Books, 2005.

Morris, Edmund. *Theodore Rex.* New York: Random House, 2001.

Tilchin, William. *Theodore Roosevelt and the British Empire: A Study in Presidential Statecraft.* New York: St. Martin's Press, 1997.

Weeks, William E. *John Quincy Adams and American Global Empire.* Lexington: University Press of Kentucky, 2002.

Williamson, Edwin. *The Penguin History of Latin America.* New York: Penguin Books, 1993.

WEB SITES

Library of Congress: The Monroe Doctrine

http://www.loc.gov/rr/program/bib/ourdocs/Monroe.html

Thomas Jefferson Commenting on the Monroe Doctrine in a Letter to James Monroe

http://www.mtholyoke.edu/acad/intrel/thomas.htm

U.S. State Department Info Page Regarding the Monroe Doctrine

http://usinfo.state.gov/usa/infousa/facts/democrac/50.htm

Biography of James Monroe

http://www.whitehouse.gov/history/presidents/jm5.html

Avalon Project: Complete Text of Monroe's Original Message

http://www.yale.edu/lawweb/avalon/monroe.htm

Picture Credits

INDEX

ABOUT THE AUTHOR

EDWARD J. RENEHAN JR. is the author of *Dark Genius of Wall Street, The Kennedys at War, The Lion's Pride, The Secret Six,* and *John Burroughs: An American Naturalist.* Renehan has appeared as a guest on C-SPAN, the History Channel, and PBS. He contributes to *American Heritage* and other national publications, and lives in coastal Rhode Island with his wife and two children.